Depression Kid

Kenneth T. Meredith
"The Depression Kid"

CROOKES FALLS PUBLICATIONS

GOLDEN STONE PRESS
LAKE CITY, COLORADO

PRINTED IN THE UNITED STATES OF AMERICA

© 1999 by Kenneth T. Meredith

Inquiries and orders should be directed to:

Crookes Falls Publications
P.O. Box 115
Lake City, CO 81235

ISBN 1-928590-03-9

To Harriet

My ever-loving wife
and proofreader

and Archel

For the gift of my toy truck
and dollar-twenty-nine cent
bicycle

Best Wishes

Ken

The Depression Kid

Contents

-PREFACE-

The Good Ol' Great Depression
wasn't so bad if you were a nine-year-old junkyard entrepreneur

The purpose of this book is to see the Great Depression from nineteen thirty to nineteen thirty-nine through the eyes of a child born into this era five years earlier. It is not only about Ken, the Depression Kid, but there are glimpses into his family life, which may not be unlike millions of others who lived through these difficult times. In this instance an alcoholic father served to make things worse.

My father was in many ways brilliant. As a small child I can remember him talking about an ambition to walk on the moon. When he went to California on an orange trucking run with his brother, he came back talking about the mountain pass at Banning, California, and the almost constant wind. "Someday they can harness that wind and light entire cities with it." Today that pass is covered with wind machines delivering electricity into the grid for those cities. He was a genius who could not crawl out of a bottle.

Mother was a loving Christian woman who took abuse and endured. She was the buffer, who always believed in and lived for her children.

-ONE-

Smoking Can Be Hazardous

As flames billowed up, I kicked two slats off a potato crate, tossed one to Don and yelled, "Start beating!"

I was the fire chief in command. Rank was determined by age; I was five. Don was only four and a half and, besides, it was my barn. This was not a volunteer fire department. We were pressed into emergency service by the thought that if we couldn't get the fire put out, our parents would likely beat us to death. So we frantically began beating the edge of the flaming boards.

Aunt Beaut started it all. Her real name was

Beulah, but she went by the alias of Beaut. When she, Uncle Rual and their three boys showed up she smoked openly. The year was 1930. Later I surmised that she was a flapper, a carry-over from the twenties. Coal black hair, snappy brown eyes and off-color jokes are what I remember. And she openly smoked ready-made cigarettes at that.

The day after they arrived, everyone except Don and me went out in the field to dig potatoes. I know this didn't fit Aunt Beaut's flapper image, but during the Great Depression everyone had to eat. Besides, I never really saw her dig any potatoes.

Not old enough to be farm laborers, Don and I were left at the three-room farm headquarters. He suggested that the proper thing for cousins to do when left alone was to smoke. I had never thought much about it. Dad had always smoked. He rolled his own, but he never was very good at it. Some guys could roll a smoke with one hand. Like most smokers of that day, Dad was labeled by the tab hanging out of his shirt pocket. It read, "Bull Durham." Now I knew what a bull was, but only vaguely imagined what Durham might be. Anyway, smoking never tempted me until now. Aunt Beaut's cigarettes did look a lot more sophisticated to me than the manure in the cow lot where our bull lived.

We both had older brothers, and so we'd learned that whenever boys do anything bad they go hide in the barn to do it. Don *stole* a package of cigarettes out of Aunt Beaut's purse. I *got* a box of matches out of our kitchen, because I didn't steal. The barn looked like it had stood forever. Boards painted only by the weather were curled, leaving wide cracks. The large doors had long since fallen away, so that one end was left open. Towards the back were bundles of cow feed.

We opened the cigarettes, put the box of matches between us and leaned back against the bundles so we could light up in luxury. That's when the trouble began. Those rascals just wouldn't light. We went through most of the matches and several cigarettes. Neither of us ever got a flame that would last after the match went out. Down to the last two matches, I made a brilliant suggestion. "We could build a fire in the fodder and get our lights from it."

We raked up a little pile and lit it. With a lot of blowing we kept it going pretty good, but we still had trouble getting a light. Those ornery cigarettes just wouldn't hold a flame.

I began to feel uneasy, afraid we might get

caught, so I swaggered to the front of the barn to look out toward the potato field. Much to my astonishment, I saw flames coming from under the floor and up the outside wall. "The barn is on fire!" I shouted in terror.

Wildly we raked the smoldering fodder out the front of the barn with the sides of our shoes. Fortunately, the legs of my coveralls never caught fire. Don was wearing short pants, and he kept complaining about the heat on his bare legs. As a fire chief I was learning fast. I told him to shut up and rake.

Next came the potato crate slats and with the help of the Lord we beat at the edges of the flaming hole in the floor and wall. Miraculously, we beat out the flames and raked the smoking fodder away from the barn. Then we ran to the house and hid under the bed. We soon got tired of that, and decided to bluff it out and hope that no one would notice.

Mom was preparing supper. She turned to my brother. "Hack, go see if you can find any eggs in the barn. The hens sometimes lay in the fodder."

Moments of agony and suspense mingled with our guilt. We didn't have to hold our collective breath long before Hack burst back into the house in panic screaming the news. "Somebody burned a big hole in the barn!"

The inquisition narrowed quickly. The trial was swift and judgment was sure.

"Annie, do you have a sharp butcher knife?" Aunt Beaut asked.

I feared for Don's life!

She went out in the yard and cut a willow switch, small enough that it would not bruise, but large enough that it would not wear out too fast. Don's short pants were pulled down and he was switched on his bare bottom with the stinging willow switch. Dad's razor strop seemed more humane to me.

We drew a life-long conclusion: *Smoking can be hazardous to your health.*

-TWO-

The Bootleggers

Aunt Beaut and Uncle Rual moved to Portales. They ran a restaurant downtown. He and Dad spent a lot of time together. He was Dad's next younger brother. I guess they could be called "drinking buddies." The question might be asked how they could afford this in the middle of the Great Depression. I was not an economist at that age, but it might have something to do with the fact that they made their own booze.

My first knowledge of this was one night when Uncle Rual showed up with a gadget that stood on a pedestal and sort of a pipe ran up

to a hand-operated lever. They would fill a bottle and place a cap on it and pull down the lever. This fastened the cap tight on the bottle.

Dad was around most of the time, so I guess he drank most of what he made. The place had a small acreage where we raised potatoes and a few peanuts. There was an old one-lung pump for watering the crops. It might have been what caused Dad to drink, because I can remember him working to get it started. He would spend most of a day when he would work awhile, and then spend about the same amount of time beating on it with a pipe and cussing it.

He had quite a few words, profane, vulgar and asking God to damn it. I didn't understand if he wanted water to come out why he was so anxious to have it dammed up. Mom didn't want me to go out to the pump house with him. I think she wanted me to wait until I started to school and got my words out of a reading primer.

One day a stranger came to the house and whispered something to Dad. He got in a hurry, grabbed a shovel, ran out to the chicken yard and buried what he called his mash. It was corn and some other stuff that he would pour water over and keep in the sun 'til it kinda grew and bubbled.

He had just put the shovel away when a car drove up. This was unusual, because our place was hard to get to and few cars ever came except relatives. In the car were two men dressed in suits and one who was dressed like a policeman. He was carrying a gun.

They looked the whole place over and were about to leave when one noticed a lot of activity out in the chicken yard. The chickens seemed to be having a lot of fun digging in the freshly shoveled dirt. Some were taking dust baths and others were eating the swollen grains of corn.

The men didn't even get a shovel. They just raked around with their feet until more corn was uncovered. One got a little bottle out of his pocket and filled it with the corn. Another put handcuffs on Dad, put him in the car and drove off. They even left the rest of the corn for the chickens.

I started for the house and Mom was standing in the doorway weeping. Suddenly I recognized the seriousness of the situation and wondered if I would ever see my Dad again.

A day or so later he came back home. He said they told him that this would go on his record and to stop bootlegging. I wondered if he was going for some sort of a record, how long it would take him to win.

We found that they had arrested Uncle Rual, too. He had been selling the booze from under the counter at the restaurant.

It seems that during the Great Depression communities like Portales could not afford to keep people in jail more than a day or so, because they had to feed them.

Needing a way to make money, Uncle Rual made a deal with a creamery in Portales to buy butter wholesale and on credit. He had heard that there was a good market for it in El Paso. Somewhere he and Dad managed to get hold of an old Model-T Ford truck. On the back of it they built a big "butter box." It was sort of like a later day walk-in cooler with walls about eight inches thick stuffed with whatever they could find for insulation. It was wider than the cab of the truck and reached all the way past the frame on the rear. It must have been seven or eight feet tall.

This box they filled with butter, layered with chipped ice and they were off to El Paso! The problem was that the shortest route was over mountain roads. They went south to Roswell, then west up past Hondo, Ruidoso, through the Mescalero Indian Reservation, Alamagordo and on to El Paso.

The rig was very top-heavy. Loaded, it was difficult to drive. Coming home after getting enough money to buy booze, *they* were "loaded."

They seldom made a trip without turning the rig over at least once. Fortunately the heavy box always hit first, leaving the cab suspended in the air. They were never seriously hurt. They would hail men to help right it on its wheels, nail the box back together and be on their way.

I don't know how long they made the "butter run," because it was measured in wrecks, rather than weeks or months. They turned it over seventeen times. By then the patches on the box began to weigh almost as much as the original. When they decided that it couldn't be patched any more the butter run ended.

Uncle Rual sold the restaurant, moved to Redlands, California, bought a new truck and started hauling oranges to points east. Somewhere along about that time he stopped drinking.

A lady and her family lived across the highway and railroad tracks from us. I guess she knew a little bit about what was going on over at our place. What Jim, her son, didn't tell she could probably hear. I believe Dad could be heard for several hundred yards when raving.

She was a Christian and began to be burdened for all those kids across the tracks. Mom probably needed help more than the rest of us. Most of her family were Christians, but she received very little support from them. They were kinda mad because Mom had married Dad.

That was true of about everyone except Aunt Maude and Uncle Henry. Maude was Dad's sister and she had helped to raise him because their Mom had died when she was twelve and Dad was ten, so she became "Mom" to a bunch of boys. Uncle Henry was Mother's brother. They, like our family, had four boys and one girl, so when we all got together each double cousin had one about his own age and gender. I remember one time they came to see us and they had an old wooden hand-rocker style washer they were bringing to Mom. It was tied on the front bumper. They had bought a new gasoline powered May Tag washer. The old wooden hand-rocker was a lot better than the rub board for Mom.

There was a revival going on in town and Jim's mom invited Archel to go with them. He went on Wednesday night and was saved. Thursday night he took Dollie with him, and she also became a Christian. The same thing was repeated on Friday night when Herschel accepted Christ as Lord of his life. Saturday night Mom went, and she also found new grace in the Lord Jesus Christ. Our home was never the same because our little home now had forgiveness, grace and the love of God. Mom, especially, had newfound strength through Christ.

Sunday found all of us except Dad walking the mile and a half along the railroad tracks into town. My short legs could not reach from one cross tie to the next in one step. I can still hear my continual plea, *"Wait for me."*

-THREE-

More Hard Times

I was just six when we moved to Clovis. We lived out east of town near the Santa Fe Railroad tracks. A lot of freight trains came through. It was the first time I knew that men rode the freights. As soon as the train slowed  down coming into town they would start jumping off, because they didn't want to get caught. I guess they didn't have tickets. We often counted over a hundred that jumped off of one train. That's when I learned to count.

Since they didn't have dining cars on freight trains, the men would be hungry. Our house was one of the closest to the tracks so they would knock on our door and ask for food. If we were having a meal, Mama would invite them in. They were always polite and no one was afraid of them. Most said they were on the way to California to try to find work to feed their families back home.

With so many trains we could feed only a few. We often had little food ourselves; but if we had any, Mama would share it. I remember once she invited two men in and divided one cold biscuit between them. She made coffee thinking that would help a little.

Aunt Beaut brought a record over to our house to play it on her little hand-cranked Victrola. I don't remember but a couple of lines of the song that she thought was funny. It was about someone coming to the door, "Lady I am so hungry I could eat grass."

"Well, go around to the back of the house, the grass is a longer there." Aunt Beaut cackled out laughing, but I didn't think it was funny. I was sad because sometimes Mom didn't have anything to give. She got mad and told Aunt Beaut to take her machine and the record and leave and never bring it back! Mom was so quiet and sweet-tempered she seldom ever got mad, but when she did, at times like this I was so proud of her.

Hard times were not always bad for a family of five kids. There was always a bunch of neighbor kids hanging around, also. I don't remember any toys at that time, but the older ones improvised. They got hold of some old worn out or blown out tires. Back then most of the tires were twenty or twenty-one inchers.

We little kids could sit down inside of one and while an older kid held it we would hook our heels just inside of each bead, then tuck our heads down inside and reach behind our heads and hold the bead on either side, thus kind of protecting our heads. We would be rolled along. The most fun came when we were given a free-rolling ride down a hill for a hundred or so yards. The bigger kids used truck tires. Some rides were thrilling. You either fell out, or rode to a stop, or ended in a crash.

The car companies never knew what a great sport they killed when they popularized six hundred by sixteen-inch tires. None of us were killed, nor did we break our necks. I'll admit to some skinned elbows and knees when we fell out. Who needs toys?

One great thing happened when we lived

along the tracks. Hack was running along the side of the house when he felt the ground a little spongy. "Hey! There might be an old Indian cave under there, or maybe some bank robbers hid their money down there." He began jumping up and down. It didn't take much until the rotten boards gave way and he started sinking.

That's when I first found out what a cesspool was. Hack grabbed onto the edge of the boards and managed to keep his head above the stinking muck while he screamed for help. Fortunately Archel was nearby and pulled him out. I thought he deserved the near swim. He was a couple of years older than me and was always picking on me. Sometimes he gave me a pretty good beating. I wasn't at all sorry that he got a good dunking.

A hosing down and a bath fixed him up a bit, but he didn't smell quite like new. Mom got the worst of it because she had to wash his clothes. Some scrap boards covered the mess and we had a new pile of dirt alongside the house. If I wanted to make Hack real mad in a hurry when he couldn't fight back, like at the table or in church, I'd lean over and whisper, "You still smell like the cesspool."

Just before school started we moved into town on Ash Street. I started to school in the first grade. It was in a room of the Library building across the highway from the high school, so I only had to walk about a half-mile. I ran home for lunch the first day. Everyone gathered around me to ask me how I liked it. Embarrassed, I said, "Better'n you."

In the afternoon the teacher made us lay our heads on the desks and tried to make us take a nap. By then I was tired of school! Pouting on the way home I found a pretty good-sized kicking rock, which I kicked all the way home. Upon my arrival, my anxious clan gathered around with their same stupid question about how I liked it. "Worse'n you!"

It was then that they noticed that my dislike had brought me home with the sole of my left shoe kicked loose. In those days new shoes were scarce, so Archel took mine to a shoe-shop and got the flapping sole sewed back on for a nickel. My education was beginning to cost, and the therapy of kicking rocks had to cease.

For the most part, Christmas around our house was going to church and a big dinner afterwards with biscuits, gravy and a chicken we had raised. Everybody, even in town, had a chicken pen. After dinner we sat around seeing who could eat the most hot peppers.

Well, this Christmas was different. I had a real store-bought present. Archel had seen a store downtown where you could guess at the number of beans in a gallon jar. The closest guesser won a prize of a gift certificate. Archel won! He gave me the most precious toy of my life. It was a little stake bed heavy metal truck about a foot long. It lasted for years. Three years later when we lived on South Richardson Street on the dry Honda Creek, I spent most of my free time carving roads, garages, etc., out of the moist sand banks. Sometimes I had construction areas that ran for about a half block and carved on several levels.

The truck stayed with me and was loved by me until I went into the Army. I left it packed away in my box of precious things, which somehow got lost in my parents' moving and storage. If I can ever find another like it in an antique shop, money will be no barrier.

I don't think Dad ever did any more bootlegging, but scarce as money was, he still bought from others who were in the business. On occasion he took me with him when he made a buy. Later I thought that if the revenuers or police wanted to find the source of the booze, all they needed to do was was ask the six-year-old son of a drunk. I knew where to find all of the moonshiners within twenty miles of Clovis.

While we still lived on Ash Street Mom started making fudge and crepe paper flowers. Archel and Dollie would sell them to the railroad men down at the roundhouse tunnel when they got off work. Sometimes they would take me with them. The roundhouse was where they worked on locomotives. It was right out in the middle of the tracks. To get to it, there was a tunnel under the tracks you could walk through. We weren't allowed to come out at the roundhouse end, but I had lots of fun running back and forth. It had a nice echo, and it made a good sales place because all of the workers had to come through the tunnel to get home. They were about the only people in town who had regular jobs. Dollie was about fifteen and usually sold more than Archel because the men liked to talk to her.

That next summer Dad got a job working for one of the "truck farmers" out of town. They raised all kinds of vegetables and had a few apple and peach trees. Dad found a vacant lot downtown on Main Street where he started an open air fruit stand. Mom ran it most of the time. I spent a lot of time hanging around down there. Sometimes when we were hungry she would buy hot tamales from a Mexican who pushed his cart back and forth on Main Street, all of the time calling, "Hot tamales for sale! Hot tamales for sale!" Then he would say it in Spanish.

Sometimes Mom was able to trade fruit or vegetables for a tamale. Most of the time they cost a nickel apiece. If more of us kids were around he would sell them three for a dime, since we were "sales amigos."

During this time they built Hotel Clovis, one of the first skyscrapers in the state. It was ten stories high! Once I got to ride the elevator to the top and looked down at the people on the sidewalk. They looked just like ants. I had ridden on one elevator before when we still lived in Portales. Mom, Dad and I had taken the train to Amarillo to visit someone in the hospital. They had an elevator that took us all the way to the second floor. None of my brothers or sister had ever ridden an elevator.

Out on Uncle Henry's farm north of Clovis on the caprock, he had a new combine that had a narrow trough with little metal slats pulled by a chain. It dragged wheat up to the grain bin on top. They called it an elevator. I sure wouldn't want to ride on it.

About the time I started to the second grade we moved to ten-twenty West Seventh Street.

Our yard backed up to the West Side Elementary School. I liked it because now that we were "West Siders," all of the "East Siders" were bums.

My folks knew my second grade teacher from somewhere. I always felt that I got special treatment. I was called "Teacher's pet," but I didn't care. Only once during that year did she make me hold out my hand while she spanked it with a ruler. I don't know what I was punished for, but I know that I didn't deserve it.

A short while later we moved again. I think that Dad probably wasn't able to pay rent and that was why we moved so often. The street that was on the west side of our house ended at Seventh Street, and running on north was a country lane that led to a ramshackle three-room house that was out in the country. I have only a couple of memories from there. It had a little spring pond that was full of waterdogs. That was our water supply. There was also a little shed that we called the wood house.

One day when I came home from school I heard Mama weeping and crying out in the loudest voice I had ever heard from her. She came out of the shed about the time I arrived. She was wiping her face and eyes on her apron. Feeling I needed an explanation she said, "I was out there praying for your father." I wanted to cry too, but I said nothing.

A short time later we moved into a little one-room house with a shed for the kitchen. It had an outhouse that had at one time boasted a primitive toilet with plumbing, the kind with a high wooden tank and a pull-chain to flush. It was stopped-up, but it didn't make any difference because we couldn't afford to have the water turned on. We paid a neighbor two bits to let us carry water for the kitchen from the faucet in his back yard. Dad dug a hole and built a one-holer next to the old toilet.

Inside we had three beds in the one room with our eating table at one end. I think the saddest event was while we were moving in. Someone had helped us move and unloaded everything into the alley. Our back door opened right into it. Everyone was helping set up the beds and Mom was carrying things into the kitchen. Suddenly she began to cry. It turned out that she had a rind from a hog ham with fat on it. Someone had stolen it from the basket of food stuff. "That's all I had to flavor the gravy for our biscuits and gravy breakfast for this month." (She was always inventive enough as a cook that I never remember going hungry.)

Her tears stopped when she remembered that she had seen a man ambling down the alley when she carried her last load to the kitchen. "If he was hungry enough to steal a hog rind, then he must be worse off than we are."

-FOUR-

Mountain Life

Picacho Hill might not even be noticeable to today's seventy-mile-per-hour drivers, but way back when, it was one of the most precarious automobile passes in the state. It was where you dropped into or climbed out of the Hondo  Valley. There was a service station with a just-in-case wrecker service at the bottom. I was less than sure that we would get to the bottom unless it was by rolling end over end for about a thousand feet.

I know that this might be the frightened perceptions of a seven-year-old, but I was almost eight. Even then, I never would have seen anything to compare with Picacho Hill. It was a narrow gravel road and guard rails had not yet been heard of. It was so steep that they said some Model T Trucks often had to back up in order to have a gear low enough. I was also seeing switchbacks, which were then called hairpin curves.

If all this was not enough, Mom, Dollie and Dad were riding in the cab of our Model T Ford Truck. Hack, Hersch, Archel and I were riding on the top, not to be confused with in the back. In the back meant that all of the family belongings (I hate to call some of it furniture) filled the narrow bed of the truck to above the cab level. On top of that were three sets of bed springs and three mattresses. This was our precarious perch that accentuated the rough road, wind, and all other vehicular movements. Here clung four boys on the top. The springs may have cushioned some bumps, but think of the swinging and swaying.

Was not this the same truck that hauled the butter box and tipped over seventeen times on these same roads, mainly in the Hondo Valley?

Was not the old beaten and battered truck now five years older?

Was Dad sober or drinking? The odds were that he was drinking. He had borrowed the money from Uncle Rual to make this move. If he had money from any source or for any need he was drinking.

He had reached the depths of drink and despair in Clovis and was in a delirium a good part of the time. He caught a ride with Uncle Rual, who thought we might do better in the Hondo Valley. He had found a house about four or five miles north of Ruidoso. It was was about a half mile east of the highway, just across the Hondo Creek (now called the Rio Ruidoso). It was a large square one-room log cabin with a kitchen in a shed off the back. This abode was known as the Hale Place.

The best part for us was that it was rent free. The previous occupant, I don't know if it was Mr. Hale, had become ill and despondent. He took his 30-30 hunting rifle to bed, put it under his chin and pulled the trigger. After this tragedy no one would live in the house. The story added to fear, mystery and drama for me. None of our family was superstitious.

To me the whole area was a paradise that summer. The creek was about a hundred yards from the house where we crossed the foot-log. Then it turned towards the house, made another turn and continued on down the valley.

This bridge was a log a little less than a foot across. The walking edge had been leveled a bit with an adz. This part was only about eight inches wide, so it was a bit safer to learn "Indian walk," placing one foot directly in front of the other. At each end was a post with a wire stretched across. It served as sort of a loose hand rail for the women folk to hold onto. The foot-log was a bit sporty when it rained and the river suddenly rose to where it lapped at the log.

Between the house and the creek ran an irrigation ditch. We got most of our water there. About a quarter of a mile upstream there was a spring where we could get drinking water when the creek rose and the irrigation ditch was muddy. It was a pretty long carry, but lots of kids made the work lighter.

We had a two-holer just around the edge of the hill out of sight from the back of the house. It was unbelievably better than the last place in Clovis.

The day after we moved in, a whole herd of cows and calves were brought into the corral just north of the house. It was the final event of a round-up by about six or eight real cowboys. They all wore leather vests, leather wrist cuffs, leather chaps, cowboy hats and boots. All wore six shooters tied down with a leather thong.

When I asked about their guns, one tall, lanky, weathered gunslinger gave me a big friendly smile and said. "Well, son, we don't often shoot people with them. They are mostly for coyotes and rattlesnakes, but they do keep people honest when there is a dispute over the ownership of cattle.

"The rest of what we wear is to protect us from the sun, brush, and thorns while looking for the cattle. You see those Saturday matinee cowboys like Buck Jones and Ken Maynard copy us, but they don't round up cattle in rough country like we do. In these hills it is the real thing. Now the Massey Family Singers, called the Sons of the Pioneers down in Roswell are a part of this country. I wouldn't be surprised if some of them haven't been on round-ups back early on. Bob Crosby, from down there, is mostly a rodeo rider now, but he's been on many round-ups.

I began to feel like I was a friend of real cowboys and I never left the top rail of that corral during the next two days of cutting and branding. They even gave me some mountain oysters for Mom to cook. She was a little hesitant, but food was food; and who knew where the next meal would come from?

I learned fast. With a piece of string, a hook, a willow pole and a small machine nut for a sinker I caught my first fish! It was a little six inch brook trout. The other kids joined in and we had fish to eat pretty often.

The first thing on Mom's mind was getting a garden spaded up alongside the irrigation ditch. We were soon eating radishes and leaf lettuce. Other slower growing things like peas and beans came along later. That garden was a life saver.

Dad got an hour or so of work from some of the ranchers around, but they were all living on the edge themselves and couldn't afford to hire any regular hands.

He would go into Ruidoso and look for odd jobs, but with the first fruits of any labors he would buy a pint of whiskey. This caused any further work to cease and only brought torment and verbal abuse to Mom. Back then we called it "cussin." It was loud, profane, and vulgar, combined with threats of violence.

Down on the creek bank at the closest point to our house grew a marvelous, huge cottonwood tree. The thing that made it so special was a limb about a foot across that grew out of the tree about as high as my chest; then it straightened almost level and ran across the creek. I could jump up, lie across it, and then stand up. It enabled me to walk across it to the other side of the creek and end up with a rather short jump to the far bank. Getting back was a little harder because the walkway limb was a little higher at that point, but I could jump and grab some climbing size limbs, swing my feet up around the walkway limb and scramble out on top.

I spent many pleasurable hours walking the limb above the water. I could lie on it and look for fish, or sit on it while fishing. It also gave me access to both sides of the creek for whatever roaming I wanted to do. Who could ask for anything more?

Once I roamed down stream to a place where the river came closer to the highway, but there the highway was higher than the river. There was a driveway down to a little settlement right on the river called Glencoe. It got that name because the Coes lived there. On my first visit I got acquainted with Old Man Coe. He was about seventy, but I don't know if he told me or he just seemed old.

We hit it off pretty good because he liked to talk, and he was so interesting I liked to listen. Most of his talk was about the past and if I could remember it all I could probably write a history book.

The one thing he told me every time I came to see him was emphasized with gestures. He would hold up his hand and say, "See those fingers that are missing? Well, I got them shot off when I was fighting side by side with Billy The Kid." I have had no reason not to believe him, because much of the fighting and killing in that period was actually a range war. History definitely records the Coe boys as being involved, and they were all ranchers. There were good and bad on both sides.

A couple of years later, when we were living in Roswell, Old Man Coe came to town to see the first Billy The Kid movie. I was told by friends who were there that about half way through he got up on the stage in front of the screen, waved his hands and shouted, "Stop the movie! Stop the movie! Stop the movie! This is all lies! This is all lies. This is all lies!" Needless to say he was promptly escorted out.

Dad got a job planting onions that lasted about three days. All of the family joined in. Our planter tools consisted of sharp sticks used to punch holes into freshly tilled soil. We would drop a baby onion into the hole about up to its green and then press the dirt back with our foot. Mom and I worked together. She would poke the hole and I would drop the onion in (because I was closer to the ground). Then Mom would press the dirt back with her foot.

One morning I had my willow pole and was heading for my favorite fishing hole, walking along a nice trail with bushes and weeds on each side. I noticed how lovely the moist smell of the creek bottom area was. Breathing deeply made it even better.

Suddenly just a few feet in front of me I saw a beautiful black and white cat followed by four kittens that were identical with her except for size. Especially beautiful were their tails. They had long hair making them about as wide as their bodies and they were held high in the air to keep them clean. They were all silky white as if they had never touched the ground.

I had to have one of those kittens. They looked about old enough to be weaned. I was trying to decide if I should run up and grab one or slowly sneak up. My decision was made for me because the mama cat stopped and looked back over her shoulder inviting me to come closer. I don't know exactly what happened next, but suddenly my eyes were stinging and I could hardly breathe. The air was filled with such a smell or stink that it was about a million times worse than Hersch's smelly feet. I knew that I was about to die, so I did what all small boys do when in life-threatening danger. That is, to run for Mama crying and screaming as loud as I could.

She, not knowing what disaster had befallen me, came running to meet me. The smell met her before I did. The only fortunate turn of events was that the irrigation ditch was between us as we reached each other. Off came my clothes and I began to think that I was going to drown before she eased up on her repeated baptisms. First came a rubbing with kerosene followed by horse liniment and anything else she could find.

Neighbors heard the screaming and came running like a search and rescue squad. They had all heard or knew first hand of the perfect cure. The most frequently suggested cure was tomato juice. Our tomatoes were not ripe yet and we couldn't afford store bought canned ones.

Mrs. Payson, from across the highway said that they had a bumper crop a couple of years back and she had some left over from last year's canning. Maybe the old stuff might be even stronger. Dollie, who seemed to be fond of being around one of her boys, went home with her to bring back a half gallon jar. Mom made her promise to come straight home.

When she came home, Buff Payson was with her. I don't know if it was to spend a few more minutes with Dollie or to get in on the excitement and laugh at me. He managed to do a bit of all, only laughing at me seemed to take first place.

Hack had been up river fishing and had missed it all. When he was close enough to where he got just a faint whiff of the spicy part of the smell, he yelled, "Oh Boy! Mom's making some of that Mexican goulash."

Usually Hack, Dollie and I slept in the same bed, with me in the middle. That night and several more to follow I was shoved off to a pallet over in the far corner. In fact, they moved all the beds so there would be a far corner. Only our ugly old grey cat was forgiving enough to sleep with me. She was a real comfort, but she almost wore her tongue out and my skin off, trying to clean me up.

With the concern of our cat, it would not seem unusual that the entire family insisted that I spend about all of my waking hours playing in the creek. They even brought a sandwich for my lunch and left it lying on the foot-log. It was at the turn in the stream just beyond the foot-log that the water had swept out a pool that was about chest deep on me.

Just splashing in the water was too boring to last through this period of rejection. Having just turned eight I thought I should do something to move me towards adulthood. I was tired of all my brothers being older and with privileges I didn't receive. Here I was free of them. I was about as free as you could get. Nothing except me and the water; free even of clothing. What could I do besides splash? Suddenly it came to me: I could learn to swim.

Now there was one friend who came to visit me regularly. He was Payson's old bull dog from up beyond the highway. He was very unusual for a bull dog. His name was not so unusual, it was Bull. The odd thing was that he liked to swim. More than, that he liked to dive. Not being a retriever from birth, he had not been trained in the usual manner.

He was more of a rock hound. I could show him a rock about the size of my fist and toss it into the water and he would dive for it. He always brought up the rock I had tossed in. He never brought up a different one. If he could not find it before he ran out of breath he would come up, breathe and dive again.

We spent many happy hours together. When I decided to learn to swim there was no one to teach me. But old Bull was a good swimmer, so I watched him. With my hind legs hinged differently from his, I knew I would have to learn to kick. Bull was willing to help, so I held on to him while he pulled me around. My kick was not a completely new style, but more like a frog kick.

When it came to propelling myself with my front paws, I thought I should be able to do better than Bull because my hands were wider than his. This worked a little bit, but I couldn't hold my head above water like he could. After many tries, choking and drinking a lot of creek water, I found I could hold my breath and put my face into the water and paddle, then come up to breathe. Most of the time when I came up to breathe I would start to sink. After much trying, I finally put it all together and was swimming. I found that downstream was easier than upstream. I could start under the foot-log, swim around the deep water curve and down to where the stream widened and shallowed.

Years later I had to swim fifty yards to get one of my Scout badges. When the scoutmaster saw my unique style he almost wouldn't let me try, because he didn't think I could make it. "Why didn't you learn to swim right instead of dog paddling?"

"I guess it was because it was a dog that taught me, and he dog paddled." I passed the test.

It didn't take long until I found that my advancement towards manhood had not changed my status much. Archel was home for a visit before he was to enroll in the new Junior College at Portales.

Some of his friends showed up and they, along with my other brothers and sister, decided to climb a mountain that rose about a thousand feet above the hill in back of our house. I begged to go along, but they didn't think I could make it. I was left at home where I pouted all day. It seemed that the day would last forever. This was worse than my isolation to the creek. At least there I had old Bull.

Wouldn't you know, they came in all excited. Back on the hill just behind our house a cotton tail jumped up and ran into a hole that had been filled with rocks. Archel, hoping for fresh meat for supper was trying to dig it out. He was picking out the rocks and tossing them over a bluff beside the hole. He pulled out one and was about to toss it when he noticed that if felt different. Taking a second look, it was perfectly smooth and seemed to be shaped like an animal.

Running to the house, he placed the object on the table where we all gathered around to inspect it. It was about eighteen inches long and was fat, kinda like a pig. It had very short legs that raised it only a couple of inches above the table. It didn't have much of a neck, but the body sort of tapered off into a rather shallow face. There were two marble-sized wide-set eye sockets and a short nose with two small nose holes. The stone was unlike any we had ever seen in our area. It almost glowed. Later I heard that was called "translucent".

Dad said he thought he knew someone in Ruidoso who might know something about it. He took it to town and did find someone so interested they traded him a pint of whiskey for it.

About thirty years later while visiting in Santa Fe, the Museum was having a display of Indian artifacts at the Palace of the Governors. There on prominent display was our find, or one exactly like it. They said it was supposed to replicate a lion for strength. Two or three were known to exist. They surmised that at one time it may have had turquoise eyes. I was glad that it was in safe hands and not sitting on a shelf in a crummy bar somewhere. (See Epilogue)

Tinnie was down river about ten or fifteen miles. It had an annual rodeo that was supposed to be real good, but it didn't work out that way for us. The main parade grounds were on a rather steep slope. In fact, there was no level ground anywhere around.

As things got underway and the calf roping was in progress, one of the ropers' horses stumbled and went rear end over teakettle. On about the third flip he broke his neck. The rider was thrown clear and he was probably about the only person more sad than I was when they placed a loop around his horse's neck and dragged him off to the side.

Dad had lost all interest in the rodeo because down a couple hundred yards under a big tree he had found some drinking buddies. I don't know how or where they got the liquor but they were pretty well soused. Talk about littering your own nest. Every time they finished a bottle they would throw it down on the rocks at their feet until there was more glass than rocks.

Dad stumbled and reached out to catch himself. What he caught was the broken end of an upturned beer bottle. It appeared that he had almost cut his hand off. He was bleeding like a stuck hog. He wrapped his shirt around it and we headed for Ruidoso in the old Ford truck. It was one wild ride with Dad alternately singing and swearing, both at the top of his voice.

He drove with one hand and held the other high in the air, waving it around getting everybody near him bloody, including Mom and me. The trip was about twenty-five miles long and every moment the question was whether he would pass out from alcohol, from loss of blood, or from losing control on the narrow mountain road.

Finally, (through prayer and the help of the Lord) we reached a doctor who stitched it up. He had cut an artery and a couple of veins. The wrist was always stiff after that. Years before, when I was about two, he had fallen into a machinery pit at the Canyon, Texas power plant and had two fingers crushed off. I guess you could say that it was fortunate that it was all on his left hand. When I was about twelve he crushed the middle finger off at the middle joint while hitching a tractor to a plow. That time I think he was sober.

Needless to say, that ended any possibility of work. So we loaded the old truck and headed for Picacho Hill again.

-FIVE-

Back to the Cotton Patch

I say "back to" the cotton patch because this
wasn't the first time. It had been the means of
survival for the family several times, but my
first memory was when we were still in Portales. I wasn't much of a cotton picker at four
years of age, but that didn't keep me from
shouldering the dirty clothes bag as my sack,
and enduring the grass burs in my knees,
goat-head stickers in my bare feet, and cotton
stalks poking me in my eyes. I did get some
cotton in the sack, but I also developed an enduring hatred for the cotton patch at a very
young age. My only reprieve was a loving

mother who, when I got tired, allowed me to sleep on her sack as she dragged it down the row.

With that background stuck in my memory I was not the most thrilled child in the world when I heard we were going to Artesia, where we would stay out of school and pick cotton. That meant all of us except Archel, because he had already gone off to college.

The log cabin in the mountains was a castle compared to our quarters on the farm a couple of miles outside of Artesia. We were latecomers, and an extended family of Mexicans already occupied the converted chicken house. At least they had four walls, which was more than could be said for the one-car garage that was completely open at one end. The most solid part was the dirt floor. Boys can put up with most anything, but in retrospect I don't know how my Mom and teen-aged sister stood it.

There are few things to write about the next four months. The work was pure repetitive drudgery. I got stung by a bee trying to compete for water at the windmill.

Herschel learned how to get rid of a hive of bees. The farmer had about twenty hives just over a broken down fence from our garage palace. He and another helper were out with a more professional bee keeper. Two wore protective gear, including nets over their heads. The pro wore none. He had only fearlessness, a smoker and bee sense. He could open a hive, rob it, or put on a super and the bees considered him one of them.

Hersch thought this looked so easy he walked out where they were working, looked into an open hive and they started to rise up. This caused Hersch to exude the smell of fear. The bees knew they had a novice and they knew how to handle him. The whole hive came up in an instant swarm around his head. These warriors came for battle. Being scared to death and now fearful it might be immediate, Hersch chose his one automatic alternative. *Run!*

He didn't know where, but instinct started him towards home. Forgetting the broken down fence about ankle high, he hit it at a speed of approximately seventy-two miles per hour. Becoming airborne, he did a beautiful forward three-sixty that would win an Olympic gold medal if they ever have a bee-run-dive-and-spin event. The marvelous thing was that he came down in perfect stride and never quit running for about half a mile. The other unexplainable thing was that the bees had been trained in making a bee-line. Their aerobatics did not include Hersch's airborne maneuver. He did not get stung.

My personal events were not so noteworthy. When visiting with a friend of Dad's in Artesia, for no good reason except perhaps flavor, a dog ran up and bit me on my behind.

I made friends with a little Mexican girl about my age and was visiting with her and her family in their chicken house home. They invited me to stay for dinner, and I was fed a rolled up tortilla hot from their little tin cook stove. Thus my introduction to authentic Mexican food. One of them produced a guitar and the girl did an after-dinner dance for us.

We had one activity that was fun. About a half-mile down in a pasture there was an irrigation ditch that ran under the road through a culvert. It was about ten feet long and just big enough for us to squeeze through with our hands extended over our heads. We practiced starting up-stream, holding our breath and clearing the culvert before running out of air, getting stuck, or drowning.

One last bit of culture relating to the open end of our home was a pre-"Off" method of treating the offending hordes of mosquitos that came out before the bees went to bed. We got a

five-gallon bucket and set it in the opening
where a door or a wall should have been. This
we filled with dried cow chips and lit them.
When it smoldered enough to fill our palace
with so much smoke the mosquitos couldn't
stand it, then it was a ticklish balance as to
whether it was us or them that got driven out
first. Whoever was getting the most bites during the night usually got up and tended the
manure.

-SIX-

The Junkyard Entrepreneur

The first place we lived in Roswell was a large old farmhouse out on the west side of town. We kids knew it must be a farmhouse be-  cause it was older than any of the others around, and it still had a big barn out behind with a hay loft. There was no longer any hay, but lots of boys. The year was about 1933. Eventually streets placed the house at Third and Union.

There were no other houses west of Union, but Third Street turned into a rutted dirt road that ran a quarter to a half-mile farther before ending at the junkyard.

Now, this was not a landfill. In those days trash was burned in barrels in the alley, and garbage was either fed to the chickens or picked up and hauled to the hog farm.

The junkyard consisted mostly of old cars from the teens and early nineteen-twenties that were worn out after about thirty thousand miles and dumped into deep-walled gullies. No one had yet learned to build a car that would last a hundred thousand miles. Most didn't last half that long. The gullies were made by runoff from Six Mile Hill. It didn't rain very often, but when a gully-washer did come along there was almost no vegetation to hold the soil.

The yard had no attendant or regulations that I knew of, so I assumed ownership, and this eight-year-old began to make his mark In the world. The first thing I did was to name it *"The K. Troy Meredith Deep Gully Car Yard and Auto Cemetery."* I thought the cars that were really dead deserved respect.

Somewhere I learned that any metal that would not stick to my magnet that came out of a Model T coil box was worth more than the rest. This included copper gas lines, wiring, brass name plates, etc. Zinc met the nonmagnetic standard, but it brought the lowest price. In the pre-chrome days, however, some of the old classics like Hupmobiles, Packards, Elgins, Chandlers, Stutz-Bearcats, and so forth, were loaded with zinc trim. It was brittle and could easily be broken off with a piece of pipe.

I took my job seriously through the summer. I would leave home early carrying my lunch, and sometimes would work until dark crawling in, out and under the piles of cars.

One great day men from the Chevrolet Garage came out towing an old Model T Ford. Chevrolet garage men didn't like Fords. This Ford didn't have a body. I guess they must have gotten mad and beat it up. Boards lay across the frame where the driver sat. Instead of pushing it over the bluff, they were so mad they poured a little gasoline on the boards, set it afire and left. It's a good thing they couldn't afford much gas.

As soon as they got out of sight I ran as hard as I could towards *my car* and pulled, kicked and beat the burning boards off. Most of the gas burned out on the frame, but some oil had caught fire. Frantically I scooped large handfuls of dirt onto it until all the blaze was gone.

Then I ran to spread the word. Soon the area

was filled with brothers, cousins and neighbors. *We* had a car! Amazingly Beezer and Curt had it running by the next day. New scrap boards with an up-side-down Coca Cola box on top made the front seat. Enough were placed across the rear frame so that two rows of boys could sit back-to-back. However illegal, we paraded around town.

On Saturday, my day off, I gathered my loot into a tow sack and carried it down to a little junk shop near the Firestone Garage. It was verified by the junk man's bigger magnet, weighed, and the price computed. Pay day was at hand. Usually I made two to four bits per week to add to the family budget. Not bad for a nine-year-old junkyard entrepreneur! On top of all those riches I was now the principal owner of an automobile.

-SEVEN-

Thrill Hills

I need to say a little more about about my gullies. They were ten to twenty feet deep. I guess that most of the soil had come from Six-Mile Hill, 'cause mostly rocks are left up there.

My Deep Gully Car Yard did not use up all of the gullies. North of mine, towards where they eventually built the swimming pool, was about another half-mile-wide stretch of gullies. They reached most of the way to Spring River, only it was dry most of the time. It didn't usually have any water 'til it got down to springs the under the Missouri Street bridge.

These gullies were so close together that

there would only be about a twenty-to-thirty-foot-wide stretch of soil 'til another gully came by. They must have been owned by some older boys who had kicked and shoveled dirt off the top edges about the width of a car. The dirt that fell made a sort of ramp. They got it to where they could drive up and over to the next gully.

By the time I came along there was a whole network of roads called, "The Thrill Hills." You would go almost straight up, over, and down again. To add to the thrill was the fact that you couldn't see anyone coming over from the other side. The passengers had to watch for cars when they were at the top 'cause the driver had to be sure he was on a road going down rather than a bluff. He also had to be sure that he had another road going up the next one and not another bluff. No roller coaster was ever that much fun. One requirement was that the girls had to scream all the way.

When Archel came home from college he took us kids on some great rides in the old '28 Dodge roadster. After we got my Model T Ford on the "Hills" we had to rewire the board seats with twice as much baling wire. We still lost some boys off the back.

-EIGHT-

The Dollar Twenty-Nine-Cent Bicycle

Another great thing happened the summer that I ran the Deep Gully Car Yard as Roswell's west side entrepreneur. My oldest brother, Archel, was home from the new Junior College at Portales. He wanted to keep a secret from me until Christmas; but being good at finding junk, I discovered his stash of junk bicycle parts in one of the feed stalls in the old barn. When I dragged them out to try to sell them he had to 'fess up that he was collecting them to build me a bicycle. It wasn't much, only a frame, a sprocket and the rear wheel. The marvelous thing was that it had a New Departure brake.

In our neighborhood we were all New Departure people. That meant class. Being A New Departure person set you apart from others, like the driver of a '32 Ford V-8 was distinguished from those who still drove Chevies with solid disk wheels. It was the difference between doing eighty in second gear and twenty with fear that any faster would throw a rod.

The distinguishing bad feature was a twenty-nine inch frame. The standard for that day was a twenty-eight inch frame. Being as small as I was called for a twenty-six-inch. Some of the "Rich Kids" in town even had twenty-four inch. I didn't want one of those because I would outgrow it too fast. I knew that once I got a bike it would have to last me most of the rest of my life.

One compensating feature was that the rear wheel was for a twenty-eight inch frame. This lowered it just a bit. Even when we ended up with a front wheel that was that same size, it put me one inch closer to the ground when I fell; but this didn't shorten the pedal reach any at all.

Archel found a front wheel at the bike shop for a dime. It had about half of the spokes missing on one side and this caused it to be bent in a graceful half moon shape. He knew that part of this was due to missing spokes. The next thing he needed was a spoke tool. He got one of these used for a nickel along with a handful of rusty used spokes.

Archel went to work with the spoke wrench. After many tiring hours of loosening and tightening on opposite sides, the front wheel finally took shape, a shape all its own. He finally got it adjusted to where it wouldn't rub, but its wobble was very visible because we never had any fenders to hide it even part time.

The bike shop man was smart and generous. I can't remember his name, but it was sort of like Wright. He once mentioned his Uncle Orville from somewhere back east who also had a bike shop.

We needed tires, a front fork, an axle for the front wheel and handlebars. Most of these he let us get from his salvage pile. We bought new pedals, handlebar grips and bearings for the front fork, wheel, and main sprocket. We figured that new bearings were essential to quality. Going the route we did gave more quality than we had in looks. Steel wool helped on the handle bars, wheels and spokes.

The tires were the old fashioned high-pressure kind with no tubes. Goat head stickers were the enemy and they grew in profusion. If you have ever stepped on one while barefooted you can understand the feelings of a bike tire. The simple repair was a tube of Neverleak inserted at the valve stem. We always called it "Everleak," because its cure was not very effective. It only cared about the minor leaks. The next process was to insert some rubber bands in the hole with a special needle that you could pull out and hope that most of the bands would stay in. Then came the process of burning the excess bands back almost to the level of the tire. Sometimes it worked. If the hole was too big for the bands, then came brass plug therapy.

This worked like a molly screw principle. You would insert a hinged portion (kinda like a cuff link hinge) into the tire and hope it would open up. This would leave a little threaded brass bolt portion on the outside. Onto that you would screw a round flat brass nut about the size of a thin dime and pray that it would hold.

One of the redeeming features of a brass plug was that it was a badge of honor hanging out there for all to see. It also made sort of a rhythmic clicking sound when you rode on the sidewalk. I had three on my front tire and each was worn to a little different tone. By the different frequencies of the clicking rhythm I could use it as an audio speedometer.

My biggest problem was that it had no seat. Since the frame was twenty-nine inch I couldn't reach the pedals if we put a seat on it. We got some cotton and cotton sack canvas and wrapped it on the frame where the seat was supposed to be. We tied it down with friction tape. By sliding from one side to the other I could almost bottom out the down stroke of each pedal. I learned to give a little pull with my toes under the other pedal as it came to the top. With me sliding back and forth over the friction tape, I wasn't sure which would wear out first, me or the tape.

Sometimes I would ride with one leg sticking through the frame. It was awkward and I couldn't get much speed, but as a temporary relief it would save my friction tape spot—mine rather than the one on the bike. Being small was an asset when riding like this. Maybe that was why my big brothers often called me Runt.

Anyway, I now had wheels like no other kid in town. I was also the only one who had a car before I got my bike. This meant I could join the big boys when they had their Union Street Bike Club meetings. They always met on Saturday mornings in the old double car garage out by our barn. I don't think that there ever was a car in it. It had a dirt floor, so that made our use even more difficult. We used a lot of spread-out newspapers.

I have already mentioned the New Departure brake. It had the surest stopping ability, but having many discs that were squeezed together to effect the stop, it had to be kept very clean to avoid increased friction. The grease also had to be just the right thickness.

So, every Saturday morning we met and cleaned our brake parts. This meant taking off the back wheel and taking out the axle and all the brake guts. Besides the bearings, cones and a threaded screw-tightener, there were all of these disks, about twenty-five. Half were made with an inside flange that turned with the axle and half with little tabs that turned with the wheel. The threaded screw-tightener squeezed them together when braking, and you had disc brakes.

Bicycle people were smart! It took another thirty-five years before anyone thought of disc brakes on cars. Maybe they didn't want to clean them every Saturday morning. For our Union Street Gang it grew into a great competition.

At first it was to see who could take his

apart, wash the parts in coal oil, and get them together again with the proper amount of light grease. The reason this was important was that when free-wheeling, all these discs have to slip past each other. This may seem hard to do, but it became so easy we had to increase the degree of difficulty. That meant we did it blindfolded. Being a junkyard entrepreneur, I often had to take things apart that I couldn't see. I gained respect when I won the blindfold time trials.

Little did I know that later this training would stand me in good stead, when in the Army we had to "field strip" our rifles. After that came the training to "field strip" a machine gun. Then they did the blindfold bit just like we had done. When I won that in our company they didn't make me a general or even a PFC, but I got a pass that weekend.

Back to the garage. The proof of our work came when we would turn our bikes upside down, and using our hands, pedal for all we were worth. Then we would time how long the back wheel would coast. I think that the arm strength of the older boys gave them the advantage in this competition, but I didn't care. My dollar twenty-nine-cent bicycle had ushered me into a new phase of life.

-NINE-

Roswell's Going to Sink

A party was going on out on Six Mile Hill. About half of the population of Roswell was out there. When the wind was just right, singing, horn honking, firecrackers and assorted other noisemakers could be heard all the way into the west side of town where we lived.

"Why is everyone so happy?" was the commonly asked question.

"Roswell is going to sink!" was the answer.

Now on the surface of things it might seem strange that impending disaster would bring on such gaiety and celebration. The same thoughts might occur if you ever get to visit

Pompeii or see pictures of the mummified fig-
ures standing at a bar with an arm lifted to
take a drink as the ashes from Vesuvius en-
gulfed them.

The obvious answer is, "No one really be-
lieves it will happen."

"If they don't believe it, then why are they all
out on Six Mile Hill? A street party downtown
would have been far more convenient and with
fewer cactuses and rattlesnakes."

The build-up of tension had been going on
for weeks. A soothsayer, fortune-teller, medi-
um, mystic, seer, astrologer, (psychics hadn't
been invented yet) or whatever else she wanted
to call herself, had been broadcasting the impending disaster over the Del Rio radio station.

Now the Del Rio radio station was one of the
most powerful stations in that part of the
country. In fact, they were many times more
powerful than the government allowed. To get
away with it they snuck over into Old Mexico
and put their powerful stuff and tall towers
over there so we couldn't find them. That's
why, when they talked about Roswell sinking,
it was just like they were standing in the same
room. Like Orson Wells' broadcast about the
men from Mars, if you heard it on the radio it
had to be true. It came through loud and clear

during the count-down of days. Even our local KGFL radio station broadcast it on the news. That proved that it was true.

Before they started sinking towns they were finding things for people, especially around Roswell. At school I heard about someone who had written and told them about losing a ring. The seer broadcast that before the town sank they would find the ring. And I heard that they did, just like the radio said!

I heard a friend say that he knew of a person whose cousin was in love with a girl. He wrote to Del Rio and asked if they should get married.

"Yes, and fast!" came the answer. I don't know if it was because the town was going to sink soon or if they were facing some other disaster. The radio didn't say. This and many other true things were coming over the radio.

As people talked, they agreed that there were many things that made Roswell sinkable.

1. There were the Bottomless Lakes just about about ten miles out of town. They tried to measure them, but they always ran out of rope before they could find a bottom. Some said there was a swift river flowing between them, and the rope was just carried downstream. My dad said that he heard that a man

drowned in one and came up in another about a week later. This only proved that they were connected, not that they had a bottom. The State of New Mexico must have believed they were bottomless, because later they named them The Bottomless Lakes State Park.

2. There was Spring River. It was only dry gulleys out where I had my old car cemetery. At the edge of town they graded it into one gully and it ran through a park. The W.P.A. men rocked up the sides and the bottom, and it got a little water from rains, but down under the Missouri Street bridge water bubbled up right out of the ground. By the time it got down to where it ran under Main Street it was a pretty good river most of the time. Good enough that they named it Spring River.

3. In the mountains west of town up above Hondo, where we lived when I was eight in the log cabin that other people were afraid to live in, Hondo Creek ran right by the cabin. It was enough of a river that I learned to swim in it. When it rained it was a flooding torrent and it frequently flooded Roswell.

On the way back to Roswell at Picacho Hill, the very scary road with hairpin curves climbed out of the Hondo Valley. From there I didn't know where the Hondo Creek went.

Later in Roswell we lived at 602 South Richardson, again right on the banks of the Hondo Creek. Here it was dry as a bone. Where did all of that water go? People said It just sunk into the ground. Well, could this water all be under Roswell and cause it to sink?

A couple of times while I lived there it rained hard enough up in the mountains that in the area where the Hondo water sank into the ground, the sand could not drink it fast enough. Or maybe the underground lake was so full that it flowed on into town. They said it spread across to Spring River at the west side and flowed through downtown. Along Main Street it reached all the way from the once-dry Hondo on the south to Camp Camino on the north side of Spring River. It was almost over my head down there.

I got real scared once when I came up on a sort of suction hole where the Main Street drain grating was missing just before I got to the river bridge. I headed back for downtown where I could be a better depth gauge. Riding on the sidewalk in front of the new Post Office on Richardson Street, my bicycle was completely under water.

4. The Lost River was out north of town on the Pecos River side of the highway. It was like

small lakes about twenty feet across that appeared in the meadow. The only trouble was that they seemed to be bigger than the opening and they ran back under the sod at the edge of the water. In fact they seemed to be connected underground. You could jump on the grass out between two of them and make the water ripple on both. I didn't dare jump too hard because I was afraid they might cave in. A stick tossed into one would slowly float to the edge towards the next one.

As you followed along these, they gradually became lower than the surface of the meadow and finally became more like a stream that sort of flowed into a kind of underground cave and was called Lost River. I never could find it, but was told by the older boys that there was a cave entrance closer to the Pecos where you could climb down and walk along the stream underground.

5. Back towards town there was the Rio Berrendo. It was more like a dry canyon where it ran under the highway from Clovis, but it picked up water from springs so fast that about three miles towards the Pecos we had a great swimming hole. The river was about twenty yards wide and deep enough that you could jump off the bridge about twelve feet

high, and not hit bottom. Wilson Lee Orr would climb up on the overhead bridge timbers about ten feet higher and dive. He said he never hit bottom, either. The rest of us were too chicken to try the high-dive.

6. We had another good swimming hole out a mile and a half east of town called Three Wells. It was made by three artesian wells close together. One shot water up about six feet into the air and one about two feet. The water just barely cleared the edge of the pipe of the third. If you could get of a couple of the fellows to help balance you on the two-foot spout, you could sit on it suspended up in the air by water and bubbles.

This swimming hole was deep enough that you could dive off of rocks on the north side and dog paddle to the sandy slope on the south side. Just before you got to the deep hole there was about a two-foot waterfall you could float over.

Some years later the famous artist, Peter Hurd, liked this place so much he painted a picture here called, "Baptism at Three Wells."

7. There was another artesian well drilled out southeast of Roswell about ten or so miles. It had a pipe that was so big that I could put my face and stomach up against it and stretch my

arms as far as they could go, and I still could not reach halfway around it. At first they had no shut-off on it, and they said it shot water straight up sixty feet in the air. They also said it was the largest artesian well in the world. Almost a thousand artesian wells were drilled in and around Roswell. They had so much water they let them run all of the time. With all this water under the town, why couldn't it sink?

8. If water was not enough for Roswell to sink into, then how about a cavern? Out northwest of town on the highway to Vaughn and off towards Capitan there was a cave. I always wanted to explore it but the older boys and men wouldn't take me. "I was too little." When they explored it they took ropes and lanterns. They said they never could find the end of it, and some figured that it must be a part of the Carlsbad Caverns. If so, it ran just about right under Roswell.

Well, I had my own private cave to think about. I was hunting cottontails out on the southside of Six Mile Hill when one ran into a fairly large hole. I crawled in after him and it got more narrow, but I could see that it was getting bigger again. I didn't have a flashlight and besides, this was known as rattlesnake country. So I chickened out. Did this become a cavern that would run down under the Hondo Sink? *Anyway, I already had enough evidence for Roswell to sink.*

We had neighbors across the street who said they didn't believe it, but they stayed up almost all night sitting out on their front porch singing sad Western songs and asking questions on their ouija board.

Dad included all of us when he said, "We don't believe it!" But he drank a lot more heavily that evening and was still awake most of the night. I decided that he just didn't have all of the evidence I had gathered. I figured I might as well be prepared for the worst.

I knew that I could swim to the old barn out back. There was a large door on a track which I figured would float loose before the water got twenty feet deep. It would serve as a great raft. In the hayloft I had stored some biscuits and green onions to eat.

Just before the ten o'clock "sinking hour" came, Huck Finn and I were happily floating down the Pecos River.

-TEN-

An Old Indian Cure

"Be careful. Watch for rattlesnakes." These were the regular parting words from my mother almost every time I went out hunting for rabbits. I guess that in the area around Roswell snakes and rabbits liked the same habitat.

Just a week or so earlier we were about fifteen miles out on the highway towards Vaughn visiting my sister's newly married friend. Bored with girl talk, I decided to go for a walk outside.

"I think you had better stay and play in the house. We have seen an unusual number of rattlesnakes recently."

Now I wasn't a coward, but at times I wasn't altogether stupid either, so I decided to heed the "stay in" suggestion.

Back home I had just dropped off to sleep when I was awakened by commotion and excited adult voices punctuated by sobs and then screams of a child obviously in extreme pain. I got out of bed and circled the crowd of adults to try to get a glimpse of what was happening. They were putting a little Mexican girl to bed in our front room where Mom and Dad usually slept.

When things calmed down I found that they were half-a-mile-away neighbors of Gertrude, whom we had just visited out towards Vaughn.

You guessed it! She had been bitten by a rattlesnake and had a bandage on her thigh.

They had taken her to the hospital out on south Main Street, where they had lanced the fang marks and used a suction cup to suck out any poison they could. They said that was all they could do since most of the poison had already spread through her body. It may have been because her parents did not have any money to have her admitted.

There was not much sleep for anyone that night. I learned some realities about rattlesnake venom. Its immediate effect is the paralyzing of nerves, and this is the most dangerous. If it gets to the right place in the body its effect is to stop the breathing mechanism. For that reason the first minutes and hours are the most critical. If a person survives the paralysis, the venom spreads throughout the body, affecting about everything it gets to. Next it develops a severe and painful infection that localizes in the area around the bite.

Later as a Boy Scout, I learned that the timing from the bite to lancing and suction is critical. This was not done 'til she reached the hospital. That's probably why they said they could do nothing more.

The pastor, Rev. Walter Orr, came to pray for her and to comfort the family. Friends of the families came also to pray and comfort, so there were repeated periods of sobbing through the night. It came not only from the little girl, but from those who came to "weep with those who weep." Even I began to understand that bit of scripture better, because I was never far from tears myself.

Since we did not have a telephone, I wondered how the word had spread so quickly. No one went back to bed. I was even allowed to sit up and drink coffee with the adults.

Towards morning an older Mexican lady showed up to take over the treatment. She said she was half Mescalero Apache Indian and knew an old Indian remedy. She asked for one of the men to go out and get her the largest prickly pear cactus leaf he could find. It didn't take long because we had vacant lots all the way over to Second Street, and they were covered with prickly pears. I always hated them because they frequently stuck me when I was hunting cottontails. I was glad to know that they might be good for something.

The elderly lady now became teacher as well as doctor. She wanted others to know, because the poultice would need to be changed every hour for several days. She took a long-tined fork and stuck it into the edge of the prickly pear leaf and held it over the open flame of our cook stove to burn off the large thorns, being very careful that she also burned off the tiny stickers that grew at the base of each thorn. With this accomplished she burned it more and then scraped off the thick skin.

It was allowed to cool a bit. "Put on warm, but careful not burn her. Bite place very tender." She put it on the area of the fang marks and bandaged it in place.

"It draw out poison," she explained.

Once when she was changing the bandage I peeked at the wound. Her whole leg was swollen as big as a balloon and appeared to be rotten. The old lady stayed with her the rest of that night and all the next day. Then her parents and my mom took over. I don't know who found the lady or where she went when she left. It seemed to me that she was almost a ghost of mercy.

In about a week of hourly changing of the poultice the little girl was well enough to go home. Whether this Indian remedy worked, or whether the little five-year-old was strong enough to stand the poison we may never know. All I know was that she walked with her parents' help when she went out the door and headed back to rattlesnake country.

I never again looked at prickly pear cactus as an enemy. Indians lived with prickly pears and rattlesnakes before Roswell ever existed. So did old Mexican/Indian women and little Mexican girls.

I guess our house was sort of a haven for the snake-bitten and the beaten. At least it was only a few days later that just after midnight, Dad showed up with a badly beaten man. He only said he found him beside a road. His face was almost unrecognizable and there were big knots on the top of his head. He also reeked of alcohol. You could only be sure of that when Dad was not near him, because he reeked, also.

He was not rational enough for us to get any kind of an answer. When his shrieks of pain subsided and we would ask what happened, he had only one answer. Through his stupor he would shout, "A Model A Ford and a Chevrolet crank! A Model A Ford and a Chevrolet crank!" This was about as close to consciousness as he ever came, but he would repeat it over and over for what seemed a half an hour at a time. We assumed that he had been beaten with the crank. The only other rationale we could figure was that early Fords had a crank that was not detachable, but the Chevrolets had one that was loose after cranking, and was usually placed somewhere in the car.

He had been put in Mom's and Dad's bed, so I guess they stayed up with him for the rest of the night. After the first hour or so of the excitement I finally went back to sleep. When I woke up he was gone. I guess they used the neighbor's phone, called the police and had them come after him.

We had the wonderful old Indian cure for the little girl's snake bite, but could not do anything about the alcoholic's beating. If we had an alcohol cure we would have used it on Dad.

-ELEVEN-

Killer Rabbit

Out towards Six Mile Hill cover was sparse. Mesquite clumps protected rattlesnakes, pack rats and rabbits. These were the Great Depression days. Food was scarce in this part of New Mexico. Just west of Roswell Hack and I were hunting cottontails. During the summer Mom depended on her two youngest to supply the meat for the table.

As rabbiters we were purists: no guns. We were rock hunters, not to be confused with rock hounds. I had one rock in each hand. I was not ambidextrous, but used the right hand for instant reloading of the left. My left was a far superior weapon. I used it once on Haskel when he was pestering me. I hit him in the stomach and knocked the wind out of him. Dad whipped me with his belt. He said it was not a fair fight because I was left handed.

A cottontail, feeling insecure in the scant cover of a half-dug-out in the shade under a clump of bear grass, dashed for the nearest mesquite fortress. Hack approached with stealth. I skirted a wide circle because I knew that little rabbit would tell everyone in the thorn bush which direction to look. To know things like this you have to learn to think like a rabbit. I was sometimes called, "Runt, the Rabbit Brain." This always made me feel proud. Although I was younger than my brother I showed occasional signs of *rabbit think brilliance.* That's why I made the pincer movement. I crept all the way to the backside of the mesquite. Not many people know which is the backside of mesquite.

Timing could not have been worse. I arrived just as a giant jackrabbit, awakened by Hack and the cottontail, decided it was time to blast off for Six Mile Hill. In one desperate leap he cleared the top of the mesquite, and once airborne, reached his top flying speed of about one hundred and eighty-seven miles per hour.

(They can only run forty-five or fifty on the ground). Too late, I saw him coming with bulging eyes, ears flattened, head tilted forward so the hardest part of the skull would hit first. He had physics on his side. You know that old law about an object in motion continuing until somebody or other gets in the way. He even had Einstein behind him with the formula MC something, meaning "mass coming."

Whatever, I was struck a near mortal blow. That rabbit, all forty pounds of him, hit me just below the rib cage with the full force of a cannon ball. I was sent head over heels backwards and ended in a doubled-up knot. I couldn't breathe. I tried to cry, to groan, to make any sound that would indicate that I was still alive. I hurt! I really hurt!

If I was dead I should hear singing. Heavenly angels, that sort of thing. Unless . . . but I didn't think I'd been that bad.

Hack, not knowing that I was well along in the process of dying, laughed so hard he rolled on the ground and into a prickly pear cactus. Suddenly he was yelling in pain for both of us.

About that time I decided I might still be alive because I hurt so much. Dead people aren't suppose to hurt. Finally I began to get short gasps of air. I still think oxygen deprivation must have affected my brain before I gasped my first good breath. I lost some of my cottontail think, but I learned a lot more about jackrabbits. *I never felt brilliant again.*

-TWELVE-

The Salesman

The foretaste of Christmas around our house was smell, rather than taste . . . the fragrant aroma of a pine forest. The Christmas seasons when I was nine, ten and eleven we sold trees. Dad went to the mountains and cut them. Once I went along, not to cut, but to drag them to the truck.

One year a trucker came by and sold us his whole load at ten cents per tree. We couldn't afford to drive to the mountains and cut for that price. We didn't have a downtown lot as people do nowadays. We were not lazy sales-men. Dad would drive the truck to an area,

park, and we would work the whole neighborhood door-to-door.

My experience in selling Liberty magazines,
Cloverine Salve, and newspapers on the street
helped. I had polished my sales pitch to perfec-
tion. "Good morning, lady. You wouldn't want
to buy a Christmas tree, would you?" Years later I learned that one should never use a negative approach. I'm not so sure. Who could re-
sist the negative approach uttered in complete
innocence by a pathetic little kid with a fifteen-
cent tree under each arm, and dragging two
twenty-five-cent ones behind him?

The selling erased what would have been a
bleak Christmas at our house. My cash flow
climbed to an all-time annual high. I made
enough for nickel presents for my brothers and
sister, and a dime for each of my parents. And
then there was Jean Marie, the girl I held
hands with walking home from school. She
had sent me a wallet of genuine artificial leather from Dayton, Ohio, the previous summer. It
was embossed with a painted-on "Souvenir of
Dayton" message. I couldn't believe she had
spent so much on me.

I repeatedly scanned the aisles of "Wooley's,"
looking for just the right gift. I finally decided
on a twenty-five-cent jewelry box: not an ordi-

nary jewelry box. It was made like a fancy chest of drawers with secret compartments. Being a successful Christmas tree salesman allowed me to be generous to all whom I loved.

One of the side benefits of selling was development of character and self-assurance. These qualities were often brought into question. One challenge came when a lady answered the door almost completely undressed. All she had on that I could see was her slip.

"May I help you?" She smiled as she asked.

My self-assurance almost left me. Somehow, I stammered through the "You wouldn't want to buy" speech. I was sure that if she couldn't afford a dress, she wouldn't want to buy a tree.

"Why, yes," she replied. "Those look nice and fresh." She patted herself where a pocket should be. "I'll have to find some change."
Now, that was the first time I ever noticed that a slip didn't have pockets. It was her patting herself there that for some reason seemed to bother me. After the transaction was completed, I had to rest to gather my self-assurance again. I was feeling kinda weak and needed to check my character to decide if I had lost it.

I pondered the educational value of selling Christmas trees. I had learned about slips and pockets, but I should have known about that all along. I had often seen my mother and older sister wearing a slip. *But on a strange woman?*

-THIRTEEN-

The Roswell Terrors

We were out on the Rio Berrendo fishing on the first day of the season. Now, the Rio Berrendo is not known as one of the world's great fisheries. A mile upstream there was no stream. It was only a gully equipped for a gully washer. As it dropped into the Pecos Valley it picked up a bit of water from springs. Where we began fishing it was three to six feet wide, and had occasional pools in its meanderings. It flowed slowly for about five miles, where it gained an identity as it joined the Pecos River. Up from the Pecos had come little sun perch, mud cat, and an occasional larger sucker.

They all had the ambition of becoming big fish in a little pond.

We had hiked out from Roswell where the dwellings on the four corners of Third and Union housed seventeen boys. Eleven of them were on this fishing expedition. Ages ranged from nine to fifteen.

Each of us was equipped with a slender new pole cut from a salt cedar clump along the bank. We had a line made of stout packaging twine. I had a half-inch machine nut for a sinker and a hook big enough to hold half a worm. I wanted one strong enough to land any good fish in the Southwest, maybe even a six-foot Pecos River gar.

As we worked downstream we came to a half-dozen houses belonging to some Rich People. We knew they were rich because they had mowed grass that ran all the way down to the Rio Berrendo. In our neighborhood people raised boys, not grass. They were poor.

Some of these Rich People didn't like eleven boys climbing their fences and fishing across their back yards. They came out to tell us so. Beezer, a cousin, had recently moved into our house along with Curt, Don and their parents. He had started going to Sunday School and decided to try some of his new-found knowledge.

"God created these fish, so they are as much ours as they are yours," he announced.

Momentarily stunned, no one was Rich enough to counter that, so one of them tried another tack.

"Fishing season doesn't start until tomorrow, boys."

We were all feeling especially religious, having a budding theologian rising in our ranks, so we let Beezer try it again.

"It ain't so," he argued. 'Tomorrow is Sunday and it is God's day when everyone goes to Sunday School and church. God would not allow fishing season to start on a Sunday."

Not a person responded. Maybe they didn't go to church. They all turned and went back to their houses. However, one of them must have been Rich enough to have a telephone. We hadn't much more than fished across their yards when a man wearing a steel gray shirt with an official looking shoulder patch came upstream. As he got closer, I could see that he had a little silver shield pinned on his shirt. He took out a pad and began writing down our names.

Now, Hack was two years older than me and was quick to perceive imminent danger. He picked up a rock about the size of a softball, stood his ground and called out in a firm voice, "Don't come any closer. I'll knock you in the head!"

Things were getting serious and fear gripped me. I was commonly called "Runt" because I was the youngest and the smallest of the litter. Since I was crying and screaming anyway, I decided to put it to use. I ran upstream to where Hersch and Curt were fishing. Between sobs I yelled, "They are going to put us all in jail! Throw down your poles and run!"

I couldn't believe how bravely the fourteen-year olds could face the music. They just walked right up to that warden and gave him their names as if a life sentence did not matter at all. Then they ratted on Hack by giving his name.

The officer said, "Put down the rock, son. I know who you are and you can't get away."

Hack blurted out, "I'm not your son!"

"Put the rock down," he admonished once more in a calm voice.

Hack took one step forward and put the rock down full force on the warden's toe. Under the circumstances it seemed better than knocking him in the head. He yelled in pain and held the foot in his hand while he did a little one-foot Indian hop dance in a near-perfect circle. He started to swear, but not wanting to contribute to the delinquency of minors, he stopped.

When the uproar subsided, he started towards his basic black Model T Ford sedan with ten of us. At that moment Beezer, who had been hiding behind a salt cedar, decided to make his escape. He ran across the road, dived under the barbed wire fence and headed straight for town.

Well, the warden loaded up the rest of us. Those he couldn't get inside stood on the running boards. Hersch and Curt sat on the front fenders, their legs straddling the headlights.

He drove leisurely around the section line roads (a section is one mile square) to a point that intersected the fugitive's path. When Beezer saw us he turned and began running the mile again, back towards the creek. I believe he could have won the Olympic Plowed Ground Two Mile Race. We drove around again to intercept him. This time my cousin, showing great stamina and determination, turned towards town *again*, but he ran only a few steps and stopped.

Whether by brilliant judgment or sheer exhaustion I do not know, but Beezer climbed through the fence and raised both hands over his head, walked slowly to the car and surrendered bravely and with dignity.

The warden took us to the back of the court house building, where the jail and the Police Station were located. He stood outside and yelled until a properly uniformed police officer arrived. He was left to guard us while the warden went inside to gloat over his capture.

This interlude in the swift and sure procedure of justice allowed us to huddle and map out our defense without counsel. There was a unanimous vote that if fined we would "lay it out in jail."

They were evidently searching available law books over at the Busy Bee Cafe, because lunch time came and went. We considered going on a hunger strike to force them to feed us, but we were too hungry. So we ate the lunches we had taken along on our fishing trip. It wasn't much, because we had anticipated roasting suckers on a spit.

When the men finally came back from the Busy Bee, they told us that they needed to locate our parents. This was not easy, since none of the families had telephones, and some could not be located until they got off work.

The promise of a speedy trial was fulfilled just after seven o'clock that evening. We were taken up to the court room where we usually held our Boy Scout Honor Court. The charges were read:

1. Fishing out of season.

2. Fishing without a license. (Hersch and Curt were over fourteen).

3. Cutting up fish for bait. (This referred to the one six-inch mud cat someone had caught.)

4. Trespassing. (Crossing those Rich People's yards.)

Then they stated that they would drop three other charges:

1. Interfering with the duties of an officer. (My running to warn Hersch and Curt.)

2. Threatening murder and attacking an officer with a deadly weapon.

At this Hack yelled out, "Not guilty!"

3. Resisting arrest.

Here Beezer, emboldened by Hack, shouted, "I was practicing for next year's junior high track meet."

The judge rapped his gavel. "Any more outbursts like that and you will all spend the night in jail!"

Hersch courteously lifted his hand, and the judge nodded to him. " When can we eat? We are hungry."

The judge didn't answer. Instead, he stated

that each of us would be fined thirty-five dollars. He dismissed the parents, telling them to report back with the money by ten o'clock.

This was 1933 and Roswell was still in the grip of the Great Depression. All of those families combined could not have raised thirty-five dollars in a month, much less thirty-five dollars per child. No one reported back, and we again declared that we would "lay it out in jail."

Finally, around midnight they told us to go home. I guess the county could not afford to feed eleven very hungry fishermen. They evidently decided that our crime did not pay.

-FOURTEEN-

Meat on the Table

Hack and I were on our way to the Bottom-less Lakes. I was on my dollar-twenty-nine-cent bicycle, and he was on his new Monkey Ward's special. He had a paper route delivering the *Roswell Daily Record*. The job demanded a good bike, and the payments demanded about all he made. I was worried about the brass plugs in my front tire on the gravel road.

As we neared the Pecos River we passed the new C.C.C. buildings. Needing a rest, we stopped to watch the activity. The young men in the Corps worked furiously at shaping up the grounds, cutting weeds, graveling walks, and painting white stones that marked off the boundary of their new barracks home.

"Wonder if I could join up," my brother pondered. "Then I wouldn't have to go to school."

"You are only thirteen," I objected. "You have to be almost a man to join up."

"I could lie," Hack countered.

"A lie doesn't make you bigger. Besides, you'd have to quit your paper route."

"But I'd make a lot more than my paper route. I hear they pay almost as much as the Army." He mused, "Maybe I'll wait till next summer when I'll be fourteen, and then join the Army. I wouldn't have to lie as big, and I'll grow a lot by then. Curts' parents lied for him and he joined the army when he was only sixteen."

"Can I have your bicycle?" I asked, quick to show my support for his new plan.

"You can if you'll pay it out," he answered.

To that I responded with confidence, "If I get your paper route I could pay it out."

We rode on a couple of miles to the Pecos River Bridge. The Pecos wasn't much of a river at that time of year, just a small stream that meandered back and forth across the wide, sandy bottom. Occasionally over against the bank there would be a deeper pool left over from better days.

We decided to take a dip in one of the pools, so we stripped off to our shorts. Seeing movement about a half mile downstream, we decided to investigate. We ran across the alternating areas of hot and cool wet sand, splashing through water in between. We were glad to be rid of the encumbrance of our clothes. It let us run faster.

As we got closer, I suddenly put on my sand brakes. "It's two guys. One of them has a gun!" I observed with quiet fear.

"We'd better sneak around," Hack decided. He was one of the best sneakers in town, especially when sneaking up on couples in the park at night. That was our favorite sport on the way home from church on Sunday nights.

We got some salt cedars between us and the gunman and cautiously moved to within a few feet of them. The man with the rifle lifted it, and new terror gripped me!

"He's going to shoot the other guy!" I whispered.

"No, he's got it pointed at the pool. Maybe there's a dead man in there," Hack answered.

There was the crack of the rifle, and the other man exclaimed, "Ya got 'im!"

He waded into the pool, reached down, and

pulled out one of the biggest fish I had ever seen in my life.

"He's shooting fish! You can get put in jail for that."

"And if he knows we saw him, he might shoot us!" I whispered again.

"No," my brother murmured, "That shirt looks familiar. It has a shoulder patch and a badge. I think he's the game warden that caught us fishing out of season. I don't believe he is allowed to arrest himself."

"Look," I observed. "The other guy has something pinned on his shirt, too. Let's go talk to them."

We stepped out from the salt cedars, and boldness overcame fear as we approached the men.

The warden looked up. "Hello, boys. Didn't know anyone was around."

"What you shooting fish for?" Hack was never slow at getting to the point. "Couldn't you be arrested for that?"

"Well, yes," the Warden responded. "I guess I could be, normally, but we have a special permit. This man is in charge at the C.C.C. Camp. He will show the boys there how to do some river work that will create more deep pools. We're shooting these gar to give the game fish a chance."

Hack continued the inquisition. "What kind of game fish?"

"Well, about all we've got in here are carp and suckers. But we may get more mud cat and perch with the gar cleaned out."

I walked over and looked at the fish he had shot. It was one of the ugliest things I had ever seen. Then I noticed a second fish lying there.

"What are ya gonna do with the fish ya shot?" I asked.

"Toss them out for the buzzards."

Always on the lookout for something for the table, I asked, "Can we have them?"

The C.C.C. man laughed, and the warden looked surprised.

"Well, I guess so," he said.

Fearful that they might change their minds, I moved fast to secure our bounty. "Come on, Hack, let's get our fish and go."

Each was nearly four feet long and weighed about fifteen to twenty pounds, ungutted and on the hoof. We tossed them over our shoulders and headed for the bridge, our clothes and the bikes.

Then we had to learn to balance the things over the handlebars and across one leg, holding them with one hand and steering with the other.

The trip back to town was slow, tiring and difficult. We dropped the fish several times, but going through town made it worth all of our trouble. We stopped at Second and Main and attracted quite a crowd. People stared with their mouths open. *I'll bet they wished they could come to our house for fish dinner.*

Well now, at first Dad didn't seem too happy and he didn't act like he knew much about filleting gar. But he finally got with it. He nailed each of the monsters to a big cottonwood tree and used his hammer, pounding on the back of our big butcher knife to cut through the tough skin. Before he got them cleaned he'd gone through diagonals, wire pliers, bolt cutters and the hack saw.

Mom got out the pressure cooker and started canning. An observing neighbor remarked, "A little gar goes a long way."

Well, just think what our big gar did. *They lasted almost to the end of the Great Depression.*

-FIFTEEN-

Marathon Man

Beezer, Stiff, Hack and I, his little brother called "Runt," were walking down West Second towards Main Street. I was using the alias of "Runt," since that's what everyone called me anyway. A car flashed by going south on Main. It was plastered all over with signs and posters advertising the Busy Bee, Cady's, the Smoke House and the Bankhead Hotel. Hack stopped. "Hey! There goes Horace Fuller. He's the guy who's going to set the record."

"What kind of record?" Stiff looked blank. He always had a cud of tobacco, and it had stunted his growth, especially between the ears.

"Where you been? The record for driving the longest. It's all over town. Everybody knows about it."

"Well, I guess my Dad's been driving about as long as anybody. He claims he once stole the old 1906 Buick from the garage where Grandpa worked and drove it around the block. He didn't get caught, ncither."

"We're not talking about how long ago. This guy is going to drive the longest without sleep," Beezer patiently explained.

"Why would he do that?"

"Money. Why do anything?"

"Where would he get money for doing something like that?"

"Didn't you see all those signs pasted on the car? People pay him to carry their advertising around. The Chevy Garage is loaning him a car, and the Busy Bee is giving him meals. They bring food out to the curb."

"I still don't know why anyone would pay big money to have somebody carry a sign. I'd do that for two bits."

"Stiff, you just aren't famous enough to be looked at. They say everybody in the world will hear about this when he sets the record."

"For four bits I'd carry a sign all day."

"Oh, shut up and look. Here he comes back.

Guess he turned around at the hospital. Maybe he should stay close to it, especially when he starts gettin' sleepy."

Horace's marathon didn't get much attention at first, but excitement built quickly and a line of cars began to follow. After a couple of days a police car pulled in to lead the parade of Model A's, Packards, Buicks, and one Flying Cloud Reo about town. Day Three saw an ambulance fall in behind Horace, advertising St. Clare's Mortuary. On the fourth day people began to sense that history was in the making. They wanted to be a part of it. In late afternoon the parade of automobiles reached along Main from North Hill all the way to South Hill.

The foursome ran alongside Horace's Chevy for the six blocks of downtown Main, Hack leading the way, while Stiff and I struggled to keep up. We dropped off at the Spring River Bridge while the cars went on up North Hill, where they turned around. Then when Horace came back by, we would run through downtown again, yelling encouragement and slapping the fenders with our palms.

Suddenly Beezer noticed the handcuffs and chain. "Hey! They've got him chained to the steering wheel. He can't quit if he wants to!"

"Aw, that's just for show. The policeman riding with him probably has the keys."

At six o'clock the next morning I was at Cady's Cafe selling the Morning Dispatch. It was great! Hundreds of people were downtown, and papers were selling like hot dogs at the ball park. I made a buck-four bits. My usual take netted about fifteen cents or five cents per hour.

Perching on the fender of a parked car that had backed into the space, I had a grandstand view every time Horace drove by. Each time he passed I waved. Once he looked my way and nodded. I'll tell you my heart skipped a beat. Was he nodding to me, or just nodding off? The next time he came by he nodded again. He had noticed me! I didn't even care if I was called runt by everyone, even Hersch, who had started it. I was as important as all the rest of those guys. Horace had never nodded to them even when they slapped his car fenders

It was Saturday. No school. Early that morning the rest of the gang showed up at Cady's. The crowd was now cheering. Horace, my friend, had just broken the World Record! Every minute set a new goal for someone else to try for.

On the final pass through town he pulled over to the curb, hit it, and the front wheel climbed onto the sidewalk. The policeman unlocked the handcuffs. A tremendous roar went up as Horace was helped out of the car in front of Purdy's Furniture Store. He looked awful. The five-day growth of scruffy beard and the sagging bags under his watering, bloodshot eyes could be seen from fifty yards. As he started across the sidewalk his legs turned to rubber and he started to fall. Two policemen caught him and dragged him inside. Once there, they turned back toward a special bed in the show window and dropped him across it. He was already dead to the world.

A screen temporarily hid him from view. When they moved it aside minutes later he was peacefully sleeping in pajamas. Everything in sight carried an advertising sign: bed, mattress, sheets, pillows, comforter, pajamas, and on and on.

Apache raids were long gone, as were the Range Wars. Billy the Kid no longer roamed this country. But Roswell was still on the map. It had a new hero, a *world record holder.* Horace Fuller had driven one hundred and twelve hours and thirty three minutes without sleep. And was he not, even now, sawing logs in Purdy's show window for all the world to see?

-SIXTEEN-

First Aid and Banana Splits

I was lying on the floor with friends anxiously working on me. I had a splint on my leg, a tourniquet on my upper arm, my feet were elevated and head lowered as treatment for shock. A com-press was held on my abdomen for a puncture wound while I was being bandaged to hold it in place.

Had I been in a horrible accident? No! It was my turn to be the victim for our Boy Scout troop's First Aid team. We had traveled one hundred and twenty miles from Roswell to Clovis to compete in a regional tournament where one team would be selected for the state finals.

We had won over all the troops in Roswell. Until now we had been considered a kind of rag-tag bunch of Scouts. We had been together only about six months. I guess we were the rejects from other troops in town, probably by our own choice. All would deny that there was ever any discrimination, but we felt it when we would show up at a meeting where everyone else was dressed in real spiffy uniforms. In fact, as I recall, that was about the only time during the great depression that I ever felt underprivileged or sort of an outcast. Kids I knew at school and considered equals, were now all spit and polish with their uniforms and looked down their noses at us.

When this new troop was organized word got out that we would all be welcome. I guess our lack of economic status kind of bound us together. Our club met in an old abandoned house about a block up North Hill from Spring River. It had no doors and no glass in the windows. None of us had uniforms like most of the Scouts in town. Our Scoutmaster, Barney Goodman, had only two requirements:

1. That we somehow acquire a handbook.

2. We must after a reasonable time, buy a neckerchief.

This did two things for us, as I am sure that he had hoped. The neckerchief identified us as Scouts, and more particularly as a member of our troop. This was a starting place for self esteem. The handbook set out requirements for advancement. Even at the first Court of Honor we began to make our mark.

Our Scoutmaster ran a tourist court out near the old swimming pool on East Second. He gave me a job of raking leaves in order to earn four-bits for these necessities. I even eventually was able to earn enough to buy a hat.

I tell all of this to show how significant it was for our First Aid team to be chosen out of fifteen troops, to go to the Regionals. Though it was not required at the Regionals, in the local competition one of the drills was treatment for snake bite. We knew from the hand-book all about the cutting and suction as the initial procedures. To those I could add the secondary treatment from first-hand experience: "The old Indian cure" using prickly pear leaves. It did not hurt our cause.

Our Scoutmaster took the whole six-man team to Clovis in his new thirty-six Chevy.

At the regionals we came in second and did not get to go Albuquerque, but we were second place *winners* and had a trophy to prove it. If they'd had snake bite in the competition we might have won first place. But we already had a first place trophy from the Roswell competition.

This trip was a big event for all of us. I had once lived in Clovis, but most of the team had never been that far away from home. The competition lasted until after lunch time and we were all hungry. We were taken to a cafe where we could go in and sit down to eat a hamburger, and drink iced tea if we wanted.

Next, Scoutmaster Barney took us to a soda fountain where we all sat on tall stools at a high counter. Mr. Goodman pointed to a sign showing everything they had. "You can have your choice of anything you see." The biggest and most delicious-looking thing on the sign said "Banana Split," and it had a picture of one in all of its luscious glory. It was also the most expensive. As we pondered thrift, which was our custom in life, we couldn't believe that much money would or should be spent on us. Not one of us had ever tasted a banana split.

Our decision was made for us when we heard Barney shout, "Bring us seven of the largest Banana Splits you have ever made!" We were not sure he would have enough money to buy gas to get back home, but loud cheering and clapping was his reward. Talk about troop loyalty. To this day there has never been a scoutmaster who has had the kind of loyalty and devotion from six rag tag Scouts as was expressed as long as he was our leader.

-SEVENTEEN-

Jersey, The Guernsey

My mother's people were all dirt farmers. They had the grit to fight through the Dust Bowl and the Great Depression and stay put. They managed with a hog or two, a yard full of chickens and a couple of cows. Crops sometimes didn't yield enough for seed, but they always salvaged enough cracked wheat for cereal. They were survivors.

On the other hand, my Dad's family were traders, entrepreneurs and business men. They were always on the move. Restless spirits.

Now, I don't know how the switch occurred,

but my quiet Mom became the trader. I do know why. She was the mother of five children born in the late teens and early twenties. And Dad was out of work.

She had a simple dream that almost became an obsession. It was to have seven quilts ready to give to each of her children on their wedding day. In the early thirtics marriage seemed in the far distant future, but the next meal was only minutes to hours away. Practicality, common sense and love caused her to become willing to part with some of her precious possessions: quilts.

She heard about a man with goats for sale. She found him and offered some quilts for two pregnant goats. The deal was completed, and soon she had five goats, for one nanny had twin kids.

A newspaper ad sent her in search of a Guernsey cow. She was a beauty, had just *come fresh*, and gave three to four gallons of milk per day. The farmer decided five for one was a pretty good deal and he could keep the calf. Mom didn't want it, because she needed the milk it would take to feed it.

What a cow she was! Not being discriminating, we called her Jersey. Well, Jersey soon became a member of the family and supplied most of our support. We had all the good, rich milk we could drink, and there was nothing cholesterol-free about her. Cholesterol hadn't been invented yet. We let the cream rise and poured it thick and pure over our steaming cracked wheat for breakfast.

We churned the extra into butter to lavish on fragrant hot biscuits. And when we came in from play, a tall cold glass of milk hit the spot! We children were even forced to like her "health food," buttermilk and clabber. Clabber was sour curdled skim milk. Today sweetened, it is known as yogurt.

Jersey was not selfish, so we had plenty left over: some to give away, and some to sell to buy staples like sugar, which we bought in a brown paper bag. It cost a nickel a pound.

Our cow enhanced my social contacts since I delivered most of the milk. The customers were friendly folk and I often stayed to talk.

An elderly Mexican lady lived next door. I had sold her Cloverine Salve. Now she became a milk customer of mine. We talked often and one day I confessed to her that in the summer, when I had time on my hands, I sometimes helped my mother quilt. She opened a little box where she kept keepsakes and found a beautiful little sterling silver thimble. On the outer edge it was embossed with beautiful engravings.

I am sure that it must have been an heirloom, so I was surprised when she gave it to me. I treasured it for years, but it got lost in my box of keepsakes when my folks moved while I was overseas during the war.

One other person I remember clearly. He was an elderly bachelor (probably about forty) who had a small house trailer parked under a big cottonwood tree across the Hondo Creek from us. He was a good talker, and all the unique features of his tiny home fascinated me.

There was a contest to bring new people to our church on the last Sunday of a revival. I invited him and he came and sat beside me on the second row in the midst of a gang of kids. I felt very important with such a guest. He came and stood beside me when I was presented my first Bible as a prize for bringing the most new people.

The Guernsey even created a good exercise program. Milking her built grip and lower arm muscles. Churning butter by shaking a half-gallon jar gave us upper arm and shoulder strength. And walking her around the edges of town to stake her out on vacant lots built our leg muscles. We would always run home. Then we would have to run back a couple of times a day to keep her on lush grass.

Being an ecology cow she provided the lots around town with good organic soil enrichment, and no one ever complained. Yes sir, Old Jersey was a great health-food cow, and she generously gave hope and survival, not only to our family, but to many of our neighbors and friends.

-EIGHTEEN-

The Daredevil

Stiff came running up the street shouting. We couldn't tell what language he was speaking, and since I didn't know what he was saying I assumed he had learned a phrase or two in Spanish. It certainly wasn't Pig Latin, which was what all the boys in our neighborhood spoke as our native tongue. But it didn't really sound like Spanish, either. It always sounded to me like they were saying "caBETica caBETica caBETica."

Mom was so proud of me when I came home one day and told her I'd learned to speak Spanish, and then I "caBETicaed," all over the house.

Maybe Stiff was speaking in tongues or something, but I never knew that he went to the Pentecostal Church or any church for that matter.

He was grabbing at his throat and was turning blue. Hack yelled, "He's choking to death!"

Being on the Boy Scout First Aid team, he threw a half-Nelson on him, kicked his feet out from under him, and dropped him face-down on the street. Stiff lay still, whether from his head hitting the pavement or from lack of breath, I didn't know.

Hack then pounced on his back to give him artificial respiration the good old-fashioned way, by driving all the air out of him and hoping some better air would come back in. I didn't know. It had never worked when I tried it on my flat bicycle tire.

Mouth-to-mouth resuscitation hadn't been invented yet. Anyway, it would have killed old Stiff. His mouth was always so full of tobacco juice that if you blew it into his lungs he never would have breathed again. Besides, none of us would dare get that close to his mouth.

Well, about the third time Hack pounced on Stiff's back a plug about the size of a jaw breaker, popped out with a kind of high pressure "p'tooie," followed by a gurgling trickle of brown juice. As he gasped for air and began to recover, we began to understand him. It was all profane, vulgar and blasphemous, and was directed at Hack for losing his plug.

He managed to get to his feet, and found the plug over in the gutter. He wiped off the gravel, and then found a pretty good-sized cigarette snipe. Extracting the tobacco, he pressed it into his chaw and popped it into his mouth.

"Mmmmmm. Menthol. Must be one of those new Kite cigarettes. Good for colds or flu." He seemed pleased by the whole episode.

"What were you so excited about?" Beezer asked.

"When?"

"Just a moment ago, when you came charging in from town."

"Oh, yeah. I remember. Everyone in town is excited. They are all talking about it. Got a big crowd down there."

"What are they excited about?" Beezer yelled.

"Oh, nothing, really. Just some guy that's going to drive a car off the cliff into one of the Bottomless Lakes while he's standing where the back seat's s'posed to be." Everyone spoke at once.

"I don't believe it! How can he drive it if he's

standing back there?"

"Who'd be dumb enough to wreck a good car?"

"It will flip when it goes over the edge. He'll be under the car and be killed."

"The bluff on the high side of that deepest lake must be five hundred feet. He'll probably dive so deep he won't come up for a week."

"Remember the guy who drowned in one lake and came up in another one a week later?"

"I hear they're all connected to a stream that flows through the unexplored part of Carlsbad Caverns."

"What if he comes shooting up out of that big new artesian well? It's the biggest in the world, you know."

"What's he doing it for, anyway?"

"Money, I guess. They passed a hat around to get enough to buy him a car. And guess what? Someone sold them that old Model T that Runt dragged out of the dump after the Chevy garage men set it on fire. He always figured they did it 'cause it was a Ford. They gave five bucks for it."

"We were robbed!" Beezer shouted. "We sold it for two dollars and four bits, and now they are getting five for it."

"Well," Hack philosophized, "I guess we

should be pleased to be a part of such an important event in history."

"But what if he gets killed," I moaned. "I was the one that found it. I will be guilty."

"No more than those guys from the garage who set it afire and didn't stay until it burned up."

That cheered me up. I thought it was about the smartest thing I'd ever heard Stiff say.

"If he wants to really make it exciting, he should pour gas all over it and set it afire like the fire diver at the Fair," Hack suggested.

Beezer pondered a moment. "No, it's too far. The fire diver at the Fair only jumps a hundred feet. If this is five hundred, he couldn't hold his breath that long."

"I still don't see where there's any money in it."

"Remember that marathon driver? He carried signs from all the stores. Probably made a million. Well, this guy is going to do the same thing, only he will rope off a big area and charge admission. About everybody in town will want to go, just to say they were there."

"They are going to put up posters in other towns, too. And they are talking about making the Bottomless Lakes a State Park. Maybe the governor will come! Only he'd probably want to get in free."

At last the big day arrived, and the crowd was about as big as the day. I saw the ticket-takers collecting money, and wondered if they would pay to see me ride my dollar-twenty-nine-cent bicycle off the bluff. *If they did, I'd sure charge plenty, 'cause they'd have to pay for my bike.*

I didn't understand why so many of the men in the crowd had to get drunk. They were not going to jump, but I sort of hoped some of them might fall. It would serve them right and might be more fun than watching the Daredevil. Some people brought chairs from home and sat right up on the edge of the bluff.

A guy on a horse did some rope tricks, and they passed a hat for him. Someone sang, "The Star-Spangled Banner," while the high school music teacher blew a bugle. A majorette twirled her baton. She threw it up in the air and started chasing it towards the cliff. Her mother screamed, and she stopped just before she became the first diver. She cried when she saw her beautiful silver baton hit the water and sink.

The bugle sounded again, and the man started our car. They had built wooden tracks for the wheels to run in, and the steering wheel was tied with rope to keep it straight. The car started forward, and the man jumped back to the boards we had put to sit on while riding over the Thrill Hills. All went well for a few feet, and then the old Ford began to wobble in the tracks. One front wheel jumped the track, and then the other. The daredevil appeared to lose his balance, struggled to stand upright, and then leaped off the car. The old Model T continued forward and went over the bluff. It did about one and a half complete end-overs before it hit the water.

The driver got up, visibly shaken and a bit skinned up. His ticket-taking friends gathered around him. The crowd began to grow restless.

Someone yelled, "Coward! Fraud!" And soon a chant was going. One of the man's friends stepped out, holding up his hands.

"This brave man may have a broken arm. We're going to town to get him to a doctor. We will get another car, set a new date, and next time it will be free for everyone."

They got into their big black Buick and headed down to the main road. All the rest of the cars had been parked about a half-mile away. The crowd, now subdued, stood in silence and watched as the Buick became enveloped in a cloud of white alkali dust. The dust cloud followed a black spot, which soon became a tiny dot, as it raced toward the Pecos River Bridge and on to Roswell.

But the big black Buick never stopped.

-NINETEEN-

The Cable Trolley

We had never heard of ski lifts. The tram to the top of the mountain above Albuquerque had not yet been built, but youthful imagination sometimes gets ahead of science. Get about twenty cousins together as we did at a family reunion out near the caprock north of Clovis at Aunt Maude's and Uncle Henry's, and there is a pooling of ingenuity from across the country.

It was decided that a trolley should be built. The most basic need was was some altitude. The peak of the barn was rejected because the termination would be in the manure of the cow lot. The water tank on the tower above the smoke house was also turned down. There was no place to anchor the cable at the top and no platform to launch from.

The windmill tower was the most likely spot. It was not quite high enough for the most daring, but that made it about right for us little kids. There were four cousins there about my age. I was nine and a half and they were all about nine.

The windmill had a ladder to the top and this one was especially good: it had two platforms. The highest was so you could work off of it when the sucker rod had to be pulled about every two years. This was necessary to replace the leathers on the pump pulled up from the bottom of the well.

The other platform about four feet below was constructed so someone could stand on it with their head and shoulders reaching through the ladder hole in the upper platform. From there the windmill wheel could be reached. There were some summer seasons when the wind just didn't blow and the windmill wheel had to be turned by man-or boy-power. There had to be water for the house, chickens and stock.

I was hired for that job the summer I was twelve. The men were all busy in the harvest, so Rondel, my red-headed double cousin, and I alternated on thirty-minute shifts pumping water from two hundred feet down by turning the blades of this boy-powered *windless mill.*

For the trolley, its needs were rather simple. A three-eighths-inch woven steel cable was attached to the upper platform. It reached down on an experimental angle to a heavy truck axle driven into the ground. It was sort of trial and error because you wanted a ride as long as the altitude would allow. There needed to be just enough slack in the cable to let the rider make a running landing. This engineering needed to be done by a physics major or an older cousin.

A piece of three-quarter-inch pipe about a foot to eighteen inches long was placed over the cable before it was fastened. This was the *hold-onto conveyance.* Sometimes it could be thrown up the cable, but most of the time it needed to be pulled up to the rider with a piece of binder twine or top cord.

The rider at the top held onto the pipe and launched himself into space. Wheee! The ride of your life if you did not crash! We had a pretty gentle ride with a drop of about twenty-five feet from the lower platform of Uncle Henry's windmill.

Two days of success and many thrilling rides

were experienced. Some braver girls even got in on the fun. But it all came to an abrupt halt when Red was on the platform and they were trying to throw the pipe up to him. Reaching as far as he could he needed only inches more before it went sliding back down the cable. Once he almost caught it and came so close he impulsively jumped to grab it. He missed and went flying through the air with the greatest of ease. Actually he did a pretty good swan dive.

The built-in safety feature came by natural causes. The well had been drilled down in a hollow. Over the years sand had washed down until it filled in around the tower. All of the activity over the past couple of days had created a giant loose sand box. Rondel's dive must have brought him in at the exact best angle. His face ploughed sand first and then his body spread eagled so that it all absorbed the shock at the same time.

He jumped up with no broken bones, but his face was covered with blood where freckles used to be. Fearing reprisals, the older boys took him over to the cattle watering tank and cleaned his face up a bit and encouraged him to stop crying by bragging on the beauty of his dive. He wasn't in very bad shape when he was taken up and presented to the adults. Some bandages and healing salve cleared up his face in a few days. Even his freckles grew back. *But the trolley came down!!*

All was not lost. Since everyone knew that the windmill fun was over for good, I thought of another place for an extended attraction close to home and began begging for the cable. I told them that it would be useful for something at my old Gully Car Lot. It wasn't really a big fib because the new trolley site I envisioned was close to the car lot anyway. I don't really know if it was my pathetic begging or if they were proud of my enterprising nature. Anyway, I took home as loot from the reunion a roll of cable and a piece of pipe.

I have mentioned that Third Street ended at Union, but a dirt-rut road ran on down to the gulleys where all of my cars were dumped. On the north side of this road was a large grove of huge cottonwood trees, most of them taller than the windmill. They were boy-friendly, so most had already been thoroughly climbed.

We selected one where we had a good cable anchor spot just a bit higher than the windmill. To expedite faster climbing we built a ladder of scrap boards nailed to the tree in a more direct line to the launching limb. The ground anchor was a piece of scrap junk I donated from my gullies.

The ride was a bit faster than on the wind-mill, so the landing runway was shorter and you had to time it right and run faster. This only added to the degree of difficulty and creat-ed more excitement.

We had only one problem. There were wil-lows growing under most of the glidepath. When you got down to their tops they tended to grab your legs. If you ploughed through them they slowed you down. A couple of times they grabbed me so hard I couldn't hold on to the pipe and did what came to be known as an un-controlled willow crash landing. None were se-rious, but no two were alike; neither were the scratches.

Our solution was relatively simple: have a time out from riding and take a willow-break session. Just break the willows under the glide path. We didn't do a very precise job, because where they were good-sized limbs we could only pull them down and break the tops. After this preliminary willowing we made a few test runs. Now instead of crashing through them we found that if we held our legs sort of hori-zontal to the cable we could glide over them.

This added another degree of difficulty. The timing from the willow break to the runway was rather critical. You had to lower your landing gear at the precise moment. We mastered this after a couple of runs and it also added to the excitement.

We had said we would set aside a Saturday morning to grub out a path under the cable, but we were having so much fun we never got around to it. It was becoming so popular kids outside of our neighborhood were coming. We had fun watching them crash until they learned the fine art. Since it was my cable, I was trying to figure how to charge admission, but the neighborhood kids already considered it theirs.

Leroy lived catercorner from our house. We didn't get to see much of him because he was blind. They said that it had happened a couple of years before we moved there. His folks were on a trip somewhere away from Roswell, and Leroy went swimming with a group of boys. There was some kind of pollution in the water that caused an infection in his eyes. This caused the blindness. The local eye doctors at that time said there was nothing they could do. A couple of other kids that were swimming with him also went blind.

Leroy did try different activities, like climbing the cottonwood trees which were behind his house. He became so familiar with some that he could climb by feel. He enjoyed the sense of height when he got up far enough that the limbs were smaller and would sway in the breeze. He seemed to have them memorized, and because he was so sensitive to feel he knew when he had reached the limit that the branches could stand. He never fell.

He heard all of the laughter across the grove at our trolley and made his way over there. We explained what we were doing and he inspected the cable at the stake and followed it up the runway as far as he could reach. He wanted to inspect the high end. He felt a little more uncertain climbing our ladder because he didn't think it felt secure enough. He used it, climbing only about the first ten feet, and then found a pathway of limbs up to our launching branch.

After feeling our pipe and sliding it back and forth, he wanted to try it. We told him that he would have to keep his feet elevated until he crossed over the willows, but needed to run as soon as he touched down. We designated someone to yell as soon as he crossed the willows so he could drop his feet.

Either the yell was too slow or he needed to drop his landing gear faster, because he was driven into the ground almost too late to run. We had a team of catchers at the bottom, and they managed to slow him enough so that there were no broken bones.

Even with the not-too-pretty landings he was thrilled and we let him repeat as many flights as he wanted. We were amazed at how he was able to learn the timing of his run until he could do about as well as the rest of us. He soon said he did not need the (not too helpful) "willow yeller." The trouble was, he had not seen the broken willow tops and the yells had not been precise enough to register in his timing mechanism. Completely on his own he made a couple of good flights.

On the third unassisted run he dropped his feet an instant too soon and plowed through the last willow top. He landed O.K. but after the second step he turned loose of the pipe, fell to the ground on his right side, and ploughed the loose dirt with his right shoulder. As soon as he stopped he grabbed his left leg. Then we began to see a bit of blood. My first thought was that he might have a broken leg with a bone sticking out.

The easiest way to get to his upper thigh was to pull his pants down. When we saw the injury, there was a stub of a willow branch about a half-inch across sticking out about an inch. We wanted to carry him home but he protested that if his parents saw it they would try to keep him housebound forever. We finally consented to pool our own First Aid skills. We found we could not pull the stob out with our fingers, so Hack got a pair of pliers out of his bicycle tool kit. One good grip by Beezer and a quick jerk and we had the offending spear in our hands. It looked like it had penetrated about an inch and a half. No bark seemed to have remained in the wound, but we all knew that we would need some disinfectant.

Dad frequently had alcohol around in half-pint bottles but he seldom turned loose of any of it until his bottle was empty. I had heard that coal oil was sometimes used, and we often had some for our lamps. Someone suggested that the bicycle club might have some in the garage. We were reminded that we had washed our brakes the previous Saturday, so it would be dirty. I volunteered to go look for some lamp oil. I knew where mom kept it in a cupboard.

I sneaked in the back door while Stiff knocked on the front and ran when mom answered it. Timing was perfect. I had a pint jar of lamp oil and was ducking under the windows as mom went back to the kitchen. Then I ran to catch up with Stiff. It wasn't hard, 'cause he ran with a kind of a lope because of his stiff leg.

Some of the older boys took over the sanitizing of the wound. Some wanted to stitch it up, but we had no cat gut. A tennis racquet was suggested, but no one had one. It was not bleeding much so we began to look for a bandage. Hack sacrificed his undershirt for the cause. It was pretty dirty, but the lamp oil could take care of that, too. All in all, we did such a good job I wondered if Leroy's blindness might have been prevented with some coal oil eye drops.

We heard that he fooled his parents that night, but the next morning his leg was so stiff that he could not get out of bed. He tried to fake how he had been wounded, but one of his brothers squealed on him.

They called Doc Hale. He was from the old school and said we had done a pretty good job, but for the sake of looks, we might have found a cleaner undershirt. Despite the fact that Leroy recovered, *the trolley came down.*

-TWENTY-

Hold All Things Loosely

Rondel and I were out on The Cap hunting cottontails with rocks. This caprock in northern New Mexico is listed as the Llano Estacado on most maps. This translates into English as the Staked Plain. To the pioneer families who staked homesteads on these plains, it was referred to as "The Cap". God allocated to the panhandle of Texas a generous portion of the Great Plains, but Texas just couldn't handle that much and a lot of it spilled over into New Mexico.

At the edge of the caprock the plains country broke abruptly and precipitously, dropping off into a five-mile-wide band of cliffs, crags, pinnacles, gullies and hills covered with pine and cedar. The colloquial name for this area was "The Breaks", and it was the nearest thing to mountains in this part of the state. It was a favorite place for recreation, wood gathering, Christmas tree cutting, hunting and such. Beyond this band the land leveled out and slowly ran on down to the Canadian River. Across the sandy river bed it rose again into high plateau ranch land until New Mexico met Colorado at Colorado's altitude.

We were working the country on top of the Cap, but we thought rabbits might be more plentiful down below. The cliff before us dropped fully two hundred feet and we started looking for a way down. About ten feet below we spied a ledge running three to four feet wide. Following this with our eyes, we saw that it pinched off to nothing about fifty feet to the right. To our left it ran a couple hundred yards, where it was broken by the head of a rock-strewn gully, suggesting a possible place where the brave or the stupid might descend.

A ten-foot jump onto the ledge might stop a lot of less dedicated rabbit hunters, but we had trained for just such an hour as this from our youth, beginning at about five years of age. We practiced jumping regularly, and worked up through the years. In ascending scale, keeping pace with age, came the brooder house, the hen house, the harness shed and the granary. Finally, we achieved the jump from the hay loft of the barn.

Rondel and I toed the line at the edge of the bluff and counted, "one-two-three-go!" This count assured that one would not jump alone and have the other chicken out. Only the most yellow-bellied coward would fail to jump after the count. So at our "One-two-three-go!" we became airborne, hoping that our leap would not carry us beyond the ledge.

Never in my jumping history had a perpendicular ten-foot descent created such commotion. Our feet had hardly touched the stony shelf when there was squawking, a great flapping of wings and guttural hisses such as we had never heard. Unknown to us as we had viewed the ledge from above, there was a shallow cave at the bottom of the drop, about six feet deep, eight feet wide and four feet high, running back under the rim rock. There, taking shelter while waiting for the thermals to heat up, was a covey of about fifteen to twenty turkey buzzards.

The unexpected company dropping in created havoc. Their first reaction was sheer terror and they huddled together in one solid buzzard mass at the back of their cave. But in a moment or two cooler heads prevailed and they sought to break out of their prison, make the great leap into space, and soar into a freedom no mortal has ever known.

In their haste they cared not the least if they launched us into space along with them. Now, this may seem improbable to most folks. But, most folks have never alighted on a narrow ledge with their full seventy-five pounds, only to be charged by a whole herd of stampeding turkey buzzards hitting them three or four at a time. They had the advantage of their combined weight, the speed of the charge, and the pressure and wind velocity of their flapping wings. Had we been less dedicated, we would surely have been blown away.

We were true hunters at heart, and game was game. We knew well the old adage of "a bird in the hand is worth fifteen over the bluff." We each grabbed our bird. Now, twenty-five pounds of finely honed muscle and sinew rapidly becomes twice that when a buzzard begins beating you with six feet of wings, clawing you with a full supply of talons, and ripping with spurs that feel like they had been sharpened for a cock fight. All this time my bird was working my face over with a beak designed to rip a deer carcass apart.

We could have withstood all of this. We might have gotten their wings folded and held. It is also possible that we might have been able to tuck their legs between ours and hold them there. Fierce raptors can be calmed with a hood placed over their eyes. Possibly our hands could have served as a sufficient blindfold.

But they used their ultimate weapon. *They breathed on us.* Being inexperienced in some of life's finer things, I had never heard of halitosis. I had smelled clogged sewers, was at the scene when Hack fell into the cesspool, and had waded through the muck of a hog lot. Once I shot a twenty-two calibre bullet into a dead cow, bloated twice its size after two weeks in the sun. Not wanting to miss hearing the whistle of the escaping putrid gas, I made the mistake of standing too close. But never in all my life had I smelled anything to compare with a turkey buzzard's breath.

Hunting, finding and catching may be the basic and most natural instinct of man through the eons of time. But all the centuries of hunting instinct can never prepare even the bravest for the moment a buzzard exhales into your face.

Being a budding philosopher and child theologian as well as a hunter, I had long advocated that all things of this earth should be held loosely. Now I add this bit of wisdom born of experience: *"One should hold his turkey buzzard more loosely than all else!"*

-EPILOGUE-

Looking Back

Reference: THE BOOTLEGGERS

About fifty years after the incident of the bootleggers, the author and his wife, Harriet, were to have lunch with Les Van Den Berg, a business man in Durango, Colorado. Our host called and asked if he could include as his guests another couple who were in town. "In fact, they are from New Mexico. You might find it interesting to talk with them."

In an attempt to find a spot of mutual ground, the conversation went like this:

"I hear that you lived in Roswell for a time. I went to high school there in about nineteen thirty-six."

I answered, "Then you may have known my older brother and sister. That's about the time they went to Roswell High." There was then an exchange of names and no recognition was acknowledged.

A bit of embarrassment followed no memory, and she said, "Well, I should say I was more from Portales; we lived there longer."

To this I replied, "I also lived in Portales before we moved to Roswell."

" Oh, Where did you live?"

"About a half-mile out of town on the highway to Elida. It was west of the highway, across the railroad tracks."

"I don't remember anyone ever living over there."

"Well, to get to our place you had to go about another half-mile towards Elida and cross the tracks where a road ran out into a wide area of salt cedars called Poker Flats. It's where guys came to gamble. But to get to our place there was a rut road that followed the tracks back north to where we lived."

"I remember Poker Flats, but no one ever lived over there except that old bootlegger."

"That old bootlegger was my Dad!!"

I led in the roaring laughter that followed. Finally the accuser choked down more embarrassment and joined the laughter. After all, we had been town neighbors and now were well acquainted.

Reference: THE JUNKYARD ENTREPRENEUR

When I was about three years of age, before the event at the beginning of this book, we had just moved to Portales and lived in a little house somewhere out in the country. Our couch sat across a corner of a room with space behind it for me to hide stuff. I must have begun in earnest, for when Mom cleaned a week or so later, she found my treasures. The little corner was filled with old car parts. Soon I owned up to the fact that they were all mine. I remember everyone laughing and wondering how I had accumulated so much in such a short time and no one had seen me gathering it.

Then came the family announcement, "When Kenneth grows up he is going to be a Junkyard Man, for sure!"

Reference: ROSWELL IS GOING TO SINK

After I had written this story, a writer friend of mine, Clarence Adams, from my childhood days, gave me a book he had written. It was an edited edition of historic bits from a Roswell newspaper published in 1909. In it was a paragraph or so about a scare-rumor that the ground was going to open up and Roswell was going to fall into it. During my accounting of the prediction of Roswell sinking, this earlier story never surfaced. Back then radio was non-existent. It was before the Del Rio station existed. Whether the mystic promoters of my story dredged some of it up from the past, we will never know. We do now know that Roswell survived two sinkings.

Reference: INDIAN ARTIFACT

About twenty-five or thirty years after the event of Archel and his friends finding the "sacred lion," I was traveling through that part of the country. I had always been curious about exactly where it had been found.

My first task was to find our old log cabin abode. It had long since vanished, but its location stood out visibly by the outline on the soil, and its relationship to other landmarks. I started to climb the hill in back of the cabin site and immediately discovered it was covered with small potsherds. I couldn't believe we had lived with them in the vicinity of our back yard and no one had ever differentiated them from the native gravel.

Proceeding on up the hill, just over the crest it leveled into about a five-acre plot, with a gentle flat slope leading back to rougher country. As I studied it, the first thing that came to my attention was a series of about a dozen depressions spread around the area. They were about eight foot across and all sloped to the center as though time had filled them all with soil. Running through this plot was a continuous meandering line that appeared to have been an ancient ditch, now also filled with the soil of time.

Convinced that I was standing on historic and sacred ground, I sought out the rabbit hole. It had been next to a bluff over which Archel said he had tossed rocks. On the south edge of the hillside plot I found a hole about eighteen inches in diameter. It was in solid rock, so it had not changed much since they dug for the cottontail. I removed a couple more smaller rocks and found some pieces of bone about six inches long and a couple of inches in diameter. I could not identify them so I placed them back and again covered them with rocks.

Curious as to whether Archel might have thrown other fetishes over the bluff, I circled to where it wasn't too steep to descend and found another surprise. The bluff was solid rock and it formed a sort of cave. The opening reached almost to the top, about fifteen feet high. It was about thirty feet across the front and perhaps as deep as it was high.

By now my observation was becoming more acute and the first thing I noticed was that the upward sloping ceiling was painted with smoke from fires of the ages. Was this a shrine or just a gathering place for the tribe as shelter from a storm? Why had their lion fetish been hidden in a hole in the rock just above? I was beginning to find more questions than answers.

One personal question was why, as an eight-year-old, had I never gone around the hill and discovered this cave? My only answer was that as a plains dry-lander, the stream demanded most of my attention.

Returning to Ruidoso in the afternoon I discovered that construction on the highway and racetrack was being delayed so that some discovered "Indian diggings" could be properly excavated. My search took me to one of the archeological specialists. Having told him my story, he warned me not to disturb anything, but he also told me one way to determine if I had truly discovered a village with pit houses.

"You can do this without damaging anything.

Select one of the typical depressions and carefully dig a small hole near the center. If it is a pit house it will have a hard packed floor about two feet below the natural surrounding surface. In the very center about six inches lower you should find a fire-pit. It will probably still have charcoal in it. Carefully put the soil back in place, removing nothing."

On the way out of my old summer home mountains, I stopped, I dug, I found the floor, I found the charcoal, I had discovered a village site! I left it as I found it.

I assume it has remained untouched. If some proper agency is interested please contact me. My prayer is that because of this writing, no reckless souvenir hunter will take advantage. My information is that this is again federal land and any illegal digging is prosecutable.

Reference: AN ALCOHOLIC FATHER

After all that has been said about my Dad and his drinking, I feel that I must add this post script. A number of times he tried to quit, but alcohol had such a grip on him that resolve usually lasted only a couple of days. I was living in the Kansas City area and Archel was a V.A. Hospital Chaplain at Wadsworth, Kansas, when we received word of his death.

We drove to Riverside, California for the services. Upon arriving back home Archel received a letter written before Dad died. It was in two parts. The first was obviously written while he was drinking, the last half while he was sober, maybe from the hospital. On the outside of the envelope he had written, "I have prayed with confidence." It is my belief that our merciful God, knowing Dad's weakness, found him in a period of sobriety, accepted him in His redeeming grace and took him Home. I expect to see him in Heaven.

Reference: MOTHER

Annie Fairy Stovall Meredith was a soft-spoken, gentle, faithful, Godly Christian. Her whole life was centered on her children. She praised our work ethic, let us know she trusted us, built our self image and believed we could do anything we attempted. She bore more abuse and deprivation than anyone should ever be asked to bear. She was killed when hit by an automobile while all four of her boys were overseas. My enduring legacy was the promise to myself at an early age that if I ever had a wife, I would never mistreat her in any way. That promise has been kept.

Portales, 1929
Back Row: Dollie, Herschel, Archel, Marion
Front Row: Kenneth, Haskel

Reference: BROTHERS AND SISTER

One might wonder what life could hold for children who grew up in such squalor and a sometimes disfunctional family.

Archel: Feeling a call of God to preach, he finished Bethany Penial College with an A.B. Degree and one year of graduate work. He worked his way through driving a motor paper route. Early in WWII he enlisted in the U.S. Army as a Chaplain and spent most of his time overseas. Upon his return to the States he entered Nazarene Theological Seminary and completed a three-year graduate degree.

He then became a Chaplain in the Veterans Administration, where he served for thirty-four years. Near the end of his term he was asked to become the Chief of Chaplains in Washington, D.C. He turned it down because he felt it would not be fair to his wife to ask her to move, and upon retirement to move again.

Concurrent with this he maintained a military relationship as a Chaplain in the National Guard, where he became a Lt. Colonel. When this unit ccased to exist he organized a Chaplains' School under the Army Reserve Corps, where he taught until his retirement.

Dollie: She was married soon after high school and raised a family of a daughter and two sons, plus foster children. One of the girls they kept and put through college. When the family was of sufficient age she went back to school and received an Associates Degree in real estate. She joined an agency in Santa Cruz, California, and immediatly became the top sales person. Within a couple of years she was a part owner of the brokerage firm.

Herschel: (Hersch) left college after a couple of years and joined the Army Air Corps, where he rapidly rose to the rank of a first sergeant. He went overseas with the first deployment of B-29 Bombers. He served in India and Okinowa.

Upon his discharge he went back to school and received a Doctor of Optometry degree. He set up his own very successful practice. He raised a lovely family of three children.

Haskel: He started to college and dropped out to Join the Army Air Corps. He served his overseas duty with the support forces in England. He brought home a British war bride. He received a job as an appraiser for the California Highway Department. He worked his way up until he was on the Appraisal Review Board in Sacramento. From there he was hired to head the Appraisal Review Board of the Bay Area Rapid Transit District, appraising properties in downtown San Francisco. Following that he transferred to the U.S. Corps of Engineers appraising properties for the proposed underground mobile missile sites in Utah and Nevada.

About the Author, "The Depression Kid"

When Ken was fourteen he left home with the tearful consent of his mother. He went to work in the wheat harvest driving a tractor pulling a combine, and stayed on through ploughing. He then moved back to Roswell where he boarded with his sister. He worked in a bakery while entering Junior High. At midterm he joined his parents at Eloy, Arizona. It was the cotton patch again, where they lived in a small wall tent in the middle of the field.

From there they followed the Grapes of Wrath dream through California. This included potato patches, lemon groves, (living under a tarp stretched across the limb of an oak tree) and pear orchards.

Moving back to Arizona, it was another fruit stand. Ken got a job at a roller rink while starting back to school. This lasted only a few days when his Dad's drinking and abuse became more than his mom could bear. She and Ken took a bus back to Redlands, California.

She did house work and he started to school, getting out at noon on a work permit. His job was refinishing grand pianos. He learned rapidly and his salary kept pace. At school they put him in the eleventh grade with, "You itinerants never know what grade you are in." Having only been to half of the ninth grade, he tried to catch up by going to Junior College in the summer and night school during the first half of his Senior year. He saw that he could not graduate with his age group, so he quit at mid-term of his Senior year. He had already enlisted in the Air Corps Reserves and adopted the philosophy, "If I am going to be killed, it won't make any difference whether I have graduated or not."

He was inducted soon after his eighteenth birthday and served in North Africa, Italy, and the South Pacific. He had been bumped from the Air Corps at induction because of the call-up of forty-two pilots who had been taught to fly at government expense.

He served with the Combat Engineers through the Rome-Arno, North-Appennines, and Po Valley campaigns. At the kick-off from the Appenines to the Po Valley he was assigned to establish an observation post under intense mortar, artillery, and sniper fire, which awarded him the Bronze Star.

After discharge he enrolled at Pasadena College and passed five college level G.E.D. tests and started as a mid-semester sophomore. Later they withdrew the thirty hours of credit, saying he had been ineligible to take the tests, hence more summer school. The bottom line is that he graduated in 1949, having been to elementary school for seven years, high school one and a half years, and college three and a half years; but there was a lot of learning in between. He received his High School diploma between his Junior and Senior year of college. He was also married to Harriet Louise Wise that same summer.

He went to Nazarene Theological Seminary

and received a three year graduate Degree in Theology. After his first year in Seminary he founded the Dundee Hills Church of the Nazarene in Kansas City North. Here he served as pastor for nine years and completed two building programs. While there he founded and the Dundee Hills Church sponsored, the Gladstone Church of the Nazarene. He then became the pastor of the First Church of the Nazarene in Lawrence, Kansas. There he was involved in the construction of a three-story educational unit. In Lawrence he also founded and the church sponsored the Victory Hills Church of the Nazarene.

While at Lawrence for five years he also attended The University of Kansas part time. He completed all the classwork requirements for a Masters Degree in Speech Communication. Before he could complete a thesis he was asked to join the administrative staff at Pasadena College in Recruiting and Estate Planning. There he completed the classwork for a Masters Degree in Adult Education. Once again he left before he wrote a thesis, and became instrumental in the founding of, and became the interim pastor of the El Morro Church of the Nazarene at Morro Bay, California.

He then became Pastor of the Santa Barbara

Trinity Church of The Nazarene. During this pastorate he obtained a real estate license and became Real Estate Consultant to Dr. Paul Benefiel, the District Superintendent of the Los Angeles District of the Church of the Nazarene. While at Santa Barbara he was also elected to the Board of Trustees (Regents) of Point Loma College in San Diego, now Point Loma University.

After a massive heart attack he retired (?) to Lake City, Colorado, where he shifted gears, obtained a Federal Energy Regulatory Commission License, designed and drew the plans for a hydro-power project. Then he served as a consultant through its construction at Crookes Falls on the Lake Fork of the Gunnison River.

Retiring again,(?) he turned to writing and has completed four books:

Yea Tho' I Walk: An Inspirational Anthology Published by Beacon Hill Press, Kansas City, Mo.

Depression Kid: Published By Crookes Falls Publications.

Tiger Tenacity: A biography of the life of Don Rodewald.

The Bed: A Civil War era novel that ends in Lake City.

The latter two are in the hands of publishers.

He also has another book half-finished, <u>Word Changes by the Im**media**cy</u>.

*Harriet and Ken Meredith at their
50th wedding anniversary
celebration
in August, 1998.*